At The Table

At the Table:

Words of Faith, Affirmation and Inspiration for LGBT Believers of Color

Compiled and Edited by

Susan A. Webley-Cox

At The Table

Glover Lane Press™
Publishers Since January 2000
www.gloverlanepress.webs.com

At the Table:
Words of Faith,
Affirmation and Inspiration for
LGBT Believers of Color Edited by Susan A. Webley-Cox™

Front Cover Design: Susan A. Webley-Cox & Azaan Kamau
Photography Provided by Susan A. Webley-Cox

ISBN-13: 978-0615820774

The Mission of Glover Lane Press is to Uplift, Empower, Elevate the Masses and Provide American Jobs. Every book published by Glover Lane Press and its many imprints, is printed and manufactured in the United States of America, ensuring and maintaining American employment.

JOHN 3:16: I AM A WHOSOEVER
Susan A. Webley-Cox

I am a whosoever

One that is despised, cast out and rejected

By a society questionably founded on democracy

The dream of 2.5 kids, a dog and a white picket fence

Surely doesn't apply

I mean, how dare I pursue to live happily?

They follow hate teachings blindly

Leaning to their own understanding

With little regard to history

(But come Sunday morning they'll take my money

After all, it's only green. I'M the one that's funny).

I am a whosoever

Yet they call me sinner and condemn me

To burn in the fiery pits of hell

For accepting how God made me

My desire to take her hand in mine

To stand in committed monogamy

At The Table

Destroys the sanctity of their version of marriage
But they can commit adultery?

Mainstreamers tell me that I can be free
Of this thing called homosexuality
But isn't trying to be something I'm not
An even graver travesty?

One's orientation does not dictate
Whether they can live holy
So I give myself permission
And use my tongue
To claim the divinity within me
Cause long before I was in the womb
My Heavenly Father knew me
In His image I was created
To love just a little differently

For God above so loved the world
That He gave up His son willingly

And I'm tired of church folk spewing the lie

That His sacrifice didn't include me

See, the last time I checked in Webster's

WHOSOEVER meant ALL and ANY

The promise of eternal life

Was not designed to be exclusionary

To receive there is only one condition required

BELIEF is all that is necessary

Those who do shall not perish

But will have life everlasting in glory

So feel free to judge me if you like

But I know what my God tells me

You will be judged the same, my friend

In that there is a certainty

I'm not looking for your acceptance,

Your approval nor your sympathy

But as God's child I have a right

To demand that you respect me

I wish to be defined by my faith

And NOT my sexuality!

John 3:16

"For God so loved the world, that he gave his only begotten Son, that whosoever believeth in him should not perish, but have everlasting life."

Dedication

This book is dedicated to the ostracized and the forgotten. To the misunderstood and the heartbroken. To those that are weary, not realizing that they still have fight in them. To my LGBT sisters and brothers who pray to be seen, but more importantly, heard.

Hold on.

Change is coming!

Acknowledgements

Keeping God first in all things - Lord, I thank you for giving me the vision for this anthology and for opening the necessary doors to bring it to fruition. You alone get the Glory!

To my best friend, my confidant, and my partner in life and in ministry, Millie - there are truly no words. You are my Aaron and Hur wrapped up in one! Thank you for loving me. Thank you for supporting me. Thank you for praying for me. Thank you for only seeing the best in me. I love you!

To Renair - thank you for never, ever allowing me to second guess myself. Thank you for checking me when I needed checking. Thank for pushing me past ME! I thank God for our friendship! I love you!

To my publisher and friend Azaan - you truly hear God! I am grateful for our connection. "*No eye has seen, no ear has heard, no mind has conceived what God has prepared for those who love him.*" (1 Corinthians 2:9) This is only the beginning! I love you!

To my biological and spiritual family, my brothers and sisters, my prayer warriors and my encouragers - your support means the world to me. I love you all from the bottom of my heart!

To my biological and spiritual children - Thank you for being a vital part of my motivation! You push me to be a better me, for YOU. I love you!

To every contributor to this anthology - Thank you for your sacrifice. Thank you for following your spirit and submitting. Thank you for your transparency. Thank you for being patient with the process. Lives will be saved because of you. I am eternally grateful!

Because of each of you, *At the Table* is. Thank you.

Table of Contents

Foreword

Some years ago a Bishop of my former church preached about a young man named Mephiboseth, who was shown mercy by King David. Mephiboseth was the grandson of King Saul and the son of Jonathan. Both were killed in battle, and David was made King. The custom in Old Testament times dictated that a new King slay the entire family of the one preceding him to ensure there was no one around to challenge his authority. When Mephiboseth's nurse heard the news, she feared for his safety -

Samuel 4:4 *"Saul's son Jonathan had a son named Mephibosheth, who was crippled as a child. He was five years old when the report came from Jezreel that Saul and Jonathan had been killed in battle. When the child's nurse heard the news, she picked him up and fled. But as she hurried away, she dropped him, and he became crippled."*

Years later it was King David's desire to show kindness to "anyone left in the house of Saul for Jonathan's sake" and told his servant Ziba to bring Mephiboseth to him. Not only did he show the young man kindness, he restored to him his entire father's land, and told him he "would eat at his table continuously" (2 Samuel 9). Despite his crippled state, Mephiboseth was set in a place of royalty.

You reading this may have been dropped by your family, friends, by all the people that were supposed to love, support and take care of you. You may have been dropped by the ONE PLACE you thought you could find refuge, because the sign on the door said "all are welcomed." Dropped by the place where you thought you could finally be rid of the anguish of living a lie, because they told you to come just as you were. Dropped by those who profess Christ but are seemingly unable to follow the Great Commandment mandated in Mark 12:30-31. Dropped by those who follow teachings blindly with no desire to study to show their own selves approved. Like Mephiboseth, you may have even thought that you were doomed to die because of who you are and who you love.

This is why *At the Table* was created. The collection of essays, poetry, testimonies and devotions in this book purposes to do for you what King David did for Mephiboseth - guide you to your place at the King's Table.

It is my prayer that this book will act as a glimmer of light in your time of darkness and bring a sense of peace to your broken spirit. I pray that it will serve as a life preserver to save you from drowning and act as a compass to help you find your way. May the words within these pages serve as hands to pick you up, arms to hold you, feet to walk beside you and a voice to affirm you. To quote a Southern Gospel classic, you are invited to "Come over here, where the table is spread and the Feast of the Lord is going on."

Please, don't keep this book to yourself. Read it, and then share it with someone you love.

God bless you!
Susan A. Webley-Cox
Editor

I AM NOT A MISTAKE

Overseer Yvonne M. Harrison
Senior Pastor, Restoration Temple Ministries
New York, NY

How can we emulate the body of Christ if we tell a segment of the population that their experience doesn't matter or that because of their sexuality they are insufficient, insignificant and/or unbiblical? In reality, the body of Christ is diverse and the body of Christ should operate in respect and love. Anything that demonizes, ostracizes, marginalizes and criticizes is far from the authentic, transparent, compassionate and loving savior of the world.

I am an African American same gender loving pastor, who is unequivocally proud of my struggle, my journey and my process to become a voice in my community, the Kingdom of Christ and the world. It hasn't been an easy journey; however, I wouldn't trade my experiences for anything in the world. I was born exactly how I am. My announcement made some things very difficult for me. When I was younger, I spent a lot of time asking God, "Why did you make me this way? Why can't I be normal like other people?" I told Him all the time that I didn't choose to be this way. I kept thinking that if only I didn't have these feelings, I would be happy. I thought that somehow God made a mistake when He made me. However, I realized that my real truth is only found in God's Word, and not in what other people say about me. I say to you, you will never find anywhere in the Bible where God calls you anything other than a child of God, minimizes your worth or concludes that you are a mistake.

Some of my favorite Scriptures are Psalm 139:14 where God says, *"I am fearfully and wonderfully made."* God tells me in Psalm 17 *"I am the apple of His eye."* In Deuteronomy 7:6 God tells me that I am *"His treasured possession."* In Philippians 4:8 God tells me to think about whatever is *"true, noble, right, pure, and lovely."* I like to think about the truth that God tells me and spend my time thinking about what God says is true. The last Scripture I want to share is Psalm 119:114 *"You are my refuge and my shield. I have put my hope in your Word."* My confidence and hope is in God. I know now that instead of being a mistake, I am the Lord's treasured possession.

Recognize that God has a plan for your life, and He created you just the way you are for His special purpose. You are not a mistake, but you are a precious gift, His treasured possession. We have a choice to believe and fill our minds with God's truth, which will change our hearts, or listen to what other people say. If you spend your time wishing you were different, you will never get around to doing those things God created you to do. God does not make any mistakes, and that's the truth! You are not a mistake! Your affirmation, your assurance is found in God's word. You are exactly what He ordained you to be and His love is inexplicable. No matter what anyone else says, or thinks, YOU are HIS! Walk in your AUTHENTICITY!

DEAR HURT
Elder Freddie Washington III
New York, NY

Dear Hurt,

It's been years since you've entered my life, and since then, we've gotten to know each other very well. It seems you've gotten pretty comfortable with me, and I have to admit that I've gotten just as comfortable with you. I guess I couldn't help it, you wouldn't allow me to get close to anyone else. All I could trust was you; all I could count on was you. I knew that if no one else was there, you would be there.

It seems that from the moment we met, I took you everywhere with me. You actually seemed to embrace me from day one. You introduced me to your friends and family and they seemed to embrace me the same way you did – anger, vengeance, depression, envy, bitterness, hate; the whole gang. You showed me a side of myself I'd never seen before. I seemed to have this strength, to be alone; strength to push everyone away.

I guess I just wanted to share you as much as I could. In the beginning, it was so I could make sure I would be ok. I told you, you were the only one I could trust. But, over time, I would give you to others without even knowing. I guess I just wanted everyone else to feel you the way I did. I wanted them all to experience that overwhelming emotion the way I did. As much as I said I didn't, the truth is I did. The reality is, while I could always count on you to be there, I didn't want you there. I just didn't know how to let you go. But, today I fell in love with forgiveness. Forgiveness saved my life. I didn't realize it, but you were killing me slowly. Forgiveness rescued me. It showed me that I didn't have to keep you around. It showed me that I didn't have to cling to you so tightly. It showed me how wrong you were for me.

It's weird. I'd heard its name uttered thousands of times, but never got to know it. Forgiveness was always a concept I imagined I understood, but today I realized I really didn't. I have no idea why we never developed a relationship. Maybe it's because you had me so blinded. But, knowing forgiveness the way I do now has changed my life.

What I love about forgiveness is that it removed all of the pain I had when I was holding onto you. Then it introduced me to happiness, self-worth, peace, and love. They're so great to me. I'm able to let others in now. I'm able to trust now. I'm able to accept others now, but more importantly, I'm able to accept myself. Forgiveness freed me.

So, this letter is just to say my goodbye. I'm letting you go for good. There's no need for you in my life anymore. And since I'm getting rid of you now, there's no need for your friends to stay. My ties to them were through you. Tell anger, vengeance, depression, envy, bitterness and hate that they won't be missed. I'm content with where I am. I'm enjoying my freedom. None of you will ever have a place here again.

But, I do want to thank you. Thank you for showing me the side of me I never wanted to see. Thank you for making me feel the pain I've felt all this time. Thank you for showing me all the baggage you come with. It let me know that no matter the experience, no matter the struggle, no matter what's said or done, I could never allow you to come back. You're not worth it and I'm too worth it. If it had not been for you, I wouldn't be so in love with forgiveness. And, if I didn't fall in love with forgiveness, I don't think I'd have ever fallen in love with me. Thank you!

Sincerely,
Me

SALVATION THROUGH A SECOND WIND
Elder Maurice L. Robinson
Rochester, NY

Life is a fight…or at least it can be. You have yourself and then you have the other forces which come to influence. Some of those influences are an immediate blessing and can be put to great use straight out of the gate. But then there are others. There are forces that come and throw us completely off. Either they are unexpected, come at a bad time or just flat out consist of moments that hurt in ways we wished we'd never have to experience. Within those moments is where the fight begins. For me, the fight began with the absence of my father and the presence of an abusive stepfather.

Every little boy wants a dad. I was no exception. Of course I had one but he was not an active part of my life. All I knew about him was his name and that he was in the military. So in my young mind, I created for him a profile. My father was a soldier overseas, fighting in wars and saving lives. My dad was a hero, a man of honor who fought fearlessly on behalf of our country and one day was going to come see about me. I wanted that to be true, I needed that to be true. So when the letters I wrote him came back, I didn't take it as 'he didn't want contact with me', I took it as 'he was too busy fighting the enemy so he didn't have time to respond.' After years of failed attempts at contact, I grew from loving this fantasy hero to hating him, not only because he wasn't there but because while he was overseas fighting the enemy, I needed him to be here with me, fighting the enemy that lived in my house.

My mother and father were not married. He was her first and she ended up getting pregnant with me. While I was developing, there was a leak in one of the amniotic sacs and the protein inside formed a band. That band somewhere got wrapped around my left hand, causing it to be deformed. My disability came as a complete shock to my mother and the family. The details surrounding my birth and the early years of my life I am still cloudy on but from what I was told, my father and my mother's then-boyfriend had problems and due to that, I never really knew my paternal family. When I was four, my mother got pregnant by her boyfriend with my little sister and the following year, they were married. My stepfather was a hardworking man who absolutely loved sports, basketball in particular. I on the other hand hated sports, it just didn't interest me, I would rather cook, sing and read. As hard as my stepfather tried, I never got into basketball or sports. He grew to resent me, not just because of my lack of interest in sports but because it dawned on him that I was not ever going to be the son that he had hoped for. Out of that resentment grew a disdain that no child should ever have to endure.

For years I suffered from emotional and physical abuse from my stepfather. To this day, my body still carries the signs of his attacks and for a long time, so did my spirit. I was always active in church, it was the only safe haven I had but after going through madness at home, I began to resent God, the church and anything that seemed to be happy because I dwelt in a dark, sad place.

Growing up with a disability was one thing, but then having to deal with these other feelings was almost too much to handle. How is it that I could go to church, try to live a good life, endure the abuse of my stepfather but then find myself being attracted to men?! I was a good Apostolic, we don't do "gay." So the battle life dealt me was dealing with a disability, dealing with abuse and the mental/emotional backlash from that, as well as dealing with my sexuality, whatever that was.

I went through depression, suicide attempts, counseling, spiritual rebellion and everything else to deal with it… Until one day while in church, a song was sung and it changed my life. During testimony service, one of the mothers hollered out and sang 'there's a war going on and you better fight!' I had never heard that song before and that night it spoke to the core of who I was. All my life I had been fighting; emotionally, spiritually, and physically. But I was fighting with no idea that there was a reason behind it all so I started to give up. Jeremiah 29:11 states *"For I know the plans I have for you," declares the LORD, "plans to prosper you and not to harm you, plans to give you hope and a future."* Everything I ever went through in my life, God knew already and made me strong enough to endure it. Not for my own sake but for the sake of those who are coming after me that will need an example of what healing and true deliverance looks like. That revelation stirred something in me that I had never felt before. A renewed sense of power, a renewed sense of purpose. I felt my second wind. For the majority of my time as a saved man and one working in ministry, I cannot begin to tell you how many times people dealing with depression have come to me for prayer and counsel. Had it not been for my experiences, I would not be able to effectively minister to them. I can speak now not from book knowledge but from honest to God moments of clarity and enlightenment. It was the second wind that allowed me to deal with my own issues and through doing so, be able to become a blessing to others that have gone through similar struggles.

My friend, I'd be lying if I said that life is great all the time because the truth is, life can suck. Situations can arise that will throw you completely off balance, things can happen that can scar you for the rest of your life, times can come that will make you question whether this life is even worth living at all. But in those times, for the love of God, fight!

Fight for the power that your past carries. Fight for the strength that your present consists of. Fight for the empowerment that your future can manifest if you allow it. Fight in the name of those that love you. Fight for those who took the time to pour into you all the love and positive energy they could muster. Fight on and should the cares of life beat you down, do whatever you can to press forward; giving up is not an option. It is in your press that the second wind is born and once that wind kicks in, it'll be a testament both to you and to those around to witness it. The first fight can finish a battle but it's the second wind that will carry you through to win the war.

WOMAN OF GOD

Stephfon L. Guidry
New York, NY

A womb filled by God

A tomb emptied by God

My God

Can bring you into

This world

Can bring you out

Elevation

An Ascension

Higher to God

A baby wrapped

In swaddling

Clothes

No Labels

Horses hay chickens

Star in the sky

Guiding leading

3 men 3 kings

Across the desert

Lost with this

Woman's gift

She submitted her body her temple

To the spirit

Without Man

A WOMAN

W/O MAN

Saved the world

She's a superhero

A gospel giver

Through pain

Through blood

Oh the Blood

Mountains and naysayers

She heard a word

A voice

An angel

Words of God

Womb of God

Birthing my dream

Weeping my tears

Anointing a Child

Searching for a child

Her family

She named him

His physical presence

Entered into our realm and

Reality through a woman

Lines words

Whispers in the night

They called her

Everything but who she is

The sin-bringer

She was tempted, the temptress

Jezebel

By a forbidden fruit

She was allowed the girth to bring sin

Into this world

And a woman

Women found

The empty tomb

WOMAN

Oh man do you see

The wonder woman

Around you

Through her submission

Of her body her temple she allows her all to

Hold the new physical manifestation

Of a spiritual predestination

Life was not

Created without design

Now life was

Not brought without

The power of God

Woman oh Woman

I thank God

He took a rib

And she

She birthed a nation

My God

I thank the

Mothers Sisters little girls aunts grandmothers

godmothers Momma

Please God you

Plan your purpose

Brought a piece of

You and made

Me I thank God

He created a woman a vessel

A pathway

He made a way

In an empty womb

Then he stepped in and Emptied the tomb

WHAT SAY THE CHURCH TO THESE THINGS?

Rev. Dawnn M. Brumfield
Chicago, IL

In her March 27, 2007 New York Times article, "For Some Black Pastors, accepting Gay members means losing others," writer Neela Banerjee tells the story of Rev. Dennis Meredith of Tabernacle Baptist Church, an African-American congregation, who "began preaching acceptance of gay men and lesbians a few years ago, he attracted some gay people who were on the brink of suicide and some who had left the Baptist faith of their childhoods but wanted badly to return." She writes, "…leaders are convinced that the Bible condemns homosexuality and that tolerance of gay men and lesbians is yet another dangerous force buffeting the already fragile black family." This scenario is not unlike many churches across the United States. There are congregations at odds with one another because of the perceived agenda of the gay and lesbian members. I do not believe there is an agenda as much as there is a desire to belong. As a member of the same-gender loving community I, too, believe that our place at the table should not be denied because of who we love.

In some black churches it is normal to see a pastor in a large, looming pulpit preaching about the dangers of sin and immorality. In many of these contexts of the black church, persons of the same-gender loving community are often categorized as sinners with lack of moral fidelity. This label is unfortunate because, in my personal experience, social ostracism is not the only reason why some lesbian, gay, bisexual or transgender (LGBT) people live life in secret. It is rather that we are shamed and dehumanized because of how and who we love. For black same-gender loving women, in particular, this problem is exacerbated by cultural norms and family expectations.

For many, the role of the woman in the black family is one of strength and courage. Throughout trials and strife the black woman is often the burden bearer of the family unit and not without problems. She often suffers through ridicule and blame for her contribution of castrating the black male. Through the Eyes of Women is a candid account of perceived roles of women and how to offer them pastoral care. Author of the essay, *The Legacy of the African-American Matriarch,* Teresa E. Snorton asserts,

> The concept of matriarch to describe the strong African-American female figure was brought into the sociological mainstream by the Moynihan report… 'matriarch' is often viewed as already having great spiritual strength and access to the spiritual resources for her own healing. She has many problems; however, traditions of faith and culture have taught her that her only recourse in this life is to look God-ward (51, 54).

It is this concept of the role of matriarch that has minimized the struggle of many African American women. The idealized black woman can feel less than normal if she has doubts concerning her sexuality and spirituality because according to the black community she is expected to be a pillar of strength and function within prescribed descriptions. Consider the family of my great grandmother, Goldia H. Smith, who, at the time of her death, was a ninety year old African American mother of three, grandmother of nine, great grandmother of eight and great-great grandmother of two. She prided herself on the fact that she never once had to live on welfare and who, though married for sixty-eight years, worked proactively as an advocate for women's role as matriarch. Mama Goldia, as she was affectionately called, was an advocate of women of strength. She intentionally raised each of her daughters to know and understand that they were expected to work, raise families and carry on the family traditions. This is not to say that she did not advocate for education, but she was clear that the expected role of women in her black family was marriage and children.

In her essay, Teresa Snorton quotes Julia A. Boyd, a psychotherapist, "This legacy of Black-womanhood-sameness is a blessing and a curse. The blessing is that in our ethnicity and our womanhood we share a sense of connection…the curse is that we're expected not to deviate from the mold of how we are supposed to be as Black women (55)." As it relates to black, same-gender loving women, their identification as lesbian would be an ultimate deviation from the mold. For many, to be a lesbian, is considered deviant behavior and certainly not appropriate behavior for women of color.

Before I turn my attention to a discussion about sexuality and the black church it is important to briefly revisit black theology and the role it played in the spiritual liberation of black people. According to James H. Cone in *Black Liberation Theology* "black theology knows no authority more binding than the experience of oppression itself" and "black people have come to know Christ precisely though oppression, because he has made himself synonymous with black oppression (120)." Put another way, black theology is written and taken from a perspective of oppression. This oppression finds itself as a point of departure for many spiritual values of the black church tradition. If this is put in terms of the LGBT community it follows that the language about, marginalization of and lack of concern for has been hurtful and damaging to an oppressed community.

In many instances the black LGBT community is socially, emotionally and spiritually oppressed. We are isolated from communities of faith, families of origin and, for some of us, caught in a web of self-hate from trying to belong and experience the radical love of Jesus that, for many of us, has been the foundation of our faith. The church, in general, would benefit from creating a different understanding of love of God, self and others. We could stand a paradigm shift that would compel us to operate with a love ethic instead of relying on words of condemnation. We should create a new culture of community and love by educating and creating space for dialogue about heterosexism. In view of Cone's articulation of black theology, "it must take seriously the reality of black people-their life of suffering and humiliation (117)." So, too, the church must take seriously the reality of the LGBT community---the suffering and humiliation.

As a woman of color it is very important that I am able to articulate how I experience life in a culture that, in many ways, refuses to affirm my existence. As a same-gender loving woman of color, it is equally significant that I can speak about myself as a person of faith who loves God *and* is committed to my life with my partner. Womanist theologians like Kelly Brown Douglas have focused on deconstructing black sexuality in order to understand its departure and influence. In her book Sexuality and the Black Church, Douglas posits that the black church and black theologians have been reluctant to discuss matters of sexuality because white racist culture has significantly contributed to black people's attitudes towards sexuality, especially toward their own sexuality (23). The black church has tremendous power and has had profound influence in constructing black culture, establishing black traditions, and teaching black mores. Yet, one of the most damaging agents in the conversation of same-gender love expressions and the black church is the black church. Given the notion of conservative preaching in many black churches there is undue condemnation that contributes to the marginalization of the LGBT community.

The church, in general and the black church in particular commits grave error in its refusal to address the issues related to same-gender loving people. For the black church community there is a need to reconstruct the weight of the minister's role in the lives of the congregants. For some, it is because of the respect for the office of Pastor and the ministry of the church, which includes the preaching of abominable behaviors, that sexuality is not welcomed topic. Peter Paris, in his book, "The Social Teaching of the Black Churches" reinforces my assertion. Black churches have "a unique history of being the single most important institutions embodying goals and purposes that pertain primarily to the welfare of black people (9)." The focus instead needs to be the concentration on God as the divine creator of human life, which includes human sexuality. Though the church relies heavily on God and the institution of the church community there is a lack of individual presence with the divine which contributes greatly to the inability for the entire church community to embrace all loving relationships including same-gender loving couples. We use scriptures like Leviticus 18:22, Genesis19:1-9, and Romans 1:26-27 to condemn persons who identify as same-gender loving. Despite the fact that these scriptures are sometimes misinterpreted or taken out of context, we quote them with such venom; we recite these passages, never giving a thought to how shaming they are. We say things like, "we love the sinner, but we hate the sin," but statements like this only further ostracize. We, black church leaders, have a responsibility to respond to the assaults on people, especially our black brothers and sisters who self-identify as gay, lesbian, bisexual, transgender, or straight ally. But too often we participate in the assaults by not engaging in purposeful dialogue and, in many cases, even refusing to create a safe space to teach, process, or reflect about sexuality. We choose instead to pretend that it doesn't exist or we become comfortable with a "don't ask-don't tell" mode of operation. That was me---it didn't---and doesn't work.

With regard to these practices, the church must be willing to critique itself. The church's response to the LGBTQ community cannot be haphazard; it should not be spoken of in a manner only to condemn. As a pastoral leader I should be intentional about exploring sexuality. It is a part of human development. And, I should be willing to do so with love, not hate and with compassion, not condemnation. Even as a religious leader, I find it difficult to manage my own faith system in a culture that is dominated by the opinions of others. But, in many ways, I am finding strength in a personal relationship with God. As a young girl, I was raised in a church culture that taught me that God so loved the world. Now, as an adult I choose to believe it and live it out. I cannot sit idly and pray that the issues will take care of themselves; I must take purposeful action against systems, programs, and language that perpetuate the problem of condemnation. Moving from condemnation to compassion is not trite work; it is work that is worth the effort. But, how do we do it?

There are many modes of pastoral care that allows a pastor to speak to the broader context of God and to reach a mass of people. Preaching is just one tool of many. It is an opportunity to offer a public perspective that can challenge the listener to engage in behavior changes and make attitude adjustments. It is also a time when the preacher can connect with the listeners by communicating a contextual gospel message that is liberative in its effect. By liberative, I don't mean preaching a "turn or burn" message. The academy has responsibly done its part to prepare pastors for the exegetical and hermeneutic work of biblical interpretation. There are classes and seminars that aptly teach the theories, principles, and methodology to sound homiletics. However, the work will be wasted if there is not careful attention given to the practice of preaching. The well-done, contextualized sermon should prompt a response to the good news---not a condemning voice---offered through the preached word. As a homiletician, I work diligently to "practice what I preach," and as a pastoral leader I commit to serving with compassion, love, grace, and wisdom.

My ministry colleagues---and perhaps others---will say I am biased, speaking and writing now only because of my personal relationship with my partner. I say perhaps there's an element of truth in that. But, when I received and accepted my Call as a minister of the gospel, I committed to God to be faithful, authentic and obedient. I am intentional about listening to God and being attentive to shifts in culture and religion. This article is evidence that the way is not always clear; it is difficult and risky facilitating conversations about sexuality, church, faith and God. Structuring or, in some cases, restructuring a belief system is painful; however, faithfulness to God and self is liberating. For me, this essay is a step in that direction.

YOU ARE VALUABLE!

"Indeed, the very hairs of your head are all numbered. Do not fear; you are more valuable than many sparrows."

Luke 12:7

AUDITION
Jerrold Yam
London, England

When I see friends sprinting to the altar,

pews slathered with a kind of pressurized calm

like the heat of summer, their legs

broken and fallen on the carpet before the cross,

I thank you for the work done

to their lives. Some shake uncontrollably,

others wail—a long languorous note

as if the soul is creeping out from the flaccid

shell of their bodies and given utterance. And when

they lay hands over me, faces wet

with divine recognition, I try to feel you churning,

gasping, in the centre of my chest

like the zygote feeding and growing on its

mother's blood. Are there people

unaccounted in your grandiose

universe plans, left out and put away

at the spark of creation? I see my friends,

so sure of salvation they can die

contented at twenty-one, how valiantly

your call is answered, how fiercely they claimed

places at your table! I will

or will not know

why you made me this way. I take my place

in pews of austere wood, a stranger

let in on charity, left to do the dirty work.

Born in 1991, Jerrold Yam is a Singaporean law undergraduate and author of *Scattered Vertebrae* (2013) and *Chasing Curtained Suns* (2012). His poems have appeared in *Poetry Quarterly*, *The New Poet*, *Third Coast*, *Washington Square Review* and elsewhere. He is the winner of the National University of Singapore's Creative Writing Competition 2011, and has been nominated for the 2013 Pushcart Prize. (http://jerroldyam.wordpress.com/)

YOU ARE WONDERFUL!

Susan A. Webley-Cox

"I praise you because I am fearfully and wonderfully made; your works are wonderful, I know that full well." Psalm 139:14 (NIV)

Take a good look at yourself in the mirror. Look at your facial features; your forehead, your eyes, nose, lips…look at the complexion of your skin, your shape, your height. Take in everything that you consider to be an imperfection; what you wish was bigger, smaller, smoother, more defined. Next, think about all of the talents and abilities that you possess that you can do especially well, things that you required no training in, you just know how to "do" them. Focus on this for a minute, and then smile!

Check you out with your unique self! You stand out, you are set apart, and you are special! No one on this planet looks like you, no one can do the things you do just like you can! That's because God made you an original, and no two of His children are alike! When God looks at you, He sees a good thing. He sees perfection in everything thing about you, because you are made in His image, and He is perfect. And when you're operating in the gifts He has given you, I can imagine His face lighting up with pride as He turns to the angels saying, "That's MY child, that's MY workmanship right there!"

This may be hard for you to do right now, but keep on practicing until you see what God sees! We all have days where we feel less than perfect; where we struggle with low self-esteem and low self-worth. This is simply a tactic of the enemy to keep us from realizing our true potential and worth in Christ. No matter what anyone says about you, tell yourself that you are beautiful, you are special, you are unique, and you are perfect! Your Heavenly Father made you, and in every sense of the word, you are WONDERFUL!

WHEN YOU KNOW IT'S REAL
Deacon Shamayara M. Woodson, MHS
Philadelphia, PA

She is gentle, she is kind...
She is affirming and caring and has always proven that my best
interest is at the center of her heart. She is stern when she needs to
be and humorous when she wants to be, who is she? She is me as I
am the reflection of them.

He is patient, he is thoughtful....
He is the whisper that guides my footsteps through the grass <u>and</u>
through the mud. When I'm stuck, he provides a way of escape, but
this sweet depiction has not always been so sweet.

I came to the conclusion I was gay when I was nineteen
years old. I wasn't the type that knew in kindergarten. I
knew I would look at women when they walked by me,
but I never equated that to being gay, until I caught
feelings for a woman who was just coming to grips with
the thought that she might be gay too. What I did know
was that there was never a separation in how I felt about
God and how God felt about me. I didn't feel fear or
shame from God, but I did feel it from the people he
charged with loving unconditionally. I knew the one
place you were supposed to be able to go to for support,
help, and prayer was the last place on earth I wanted to
be. It hurt too much to sit amongst people who despised
who I was. That wasn't hurt I wanted to endure very
often, so I kept my mouth shut. I told who I wanted on
my terms and that was it.

I became aware, spiritually, of the things around me that didn't fit into where I was growing spiritually and mentally. As my thoughts were challenged, so were the things I had been taught all my life and I found myself making a vow to God as I left my Pentecostal church, to never return if I couldn't return authentically. The lessons that my mother, grandmother and aunts had taught me were all presented to me, one after another. What I learned is the key values instilled in me were aligned with what I personally believed. God was no different. As I experienced life, I also experienced God. She was becoming real to me, not just the stories of what she did for someone else. When my heart was broken for the very first time, it was God that kept me sane on days where I didn't want to get out of the bed. When my lovers betrayed me and left me to pick up the pieces, she was there sweeping each piece up with me. God became real to me.

As I continued to grow, I could no longer deny that God wanted to use me to do something. I struggled to fit into roles that others saw me in or God ordained me through them to do, somehow forgetting to send the memo to me. I learned to trust the "feeling" I got in the bottom of my stomach that felt like nervous energy. When God felt I was ready, he began to show me my spiritual gifts. He was gentle as always until I got used to them. What I learned about God I didn't read in the Bible. She taught me as any loving, caring mother/sister would do. She teaches me through life. When I get it right, I move on and experience elevation and if I don't I remain where I am until the test is given again. I've learned to search myself for the lesson and how I can apply it to my life. I hear the messages in music, movies, Facebook statuses, flowers blowing in the wind… everywhere. I love the fact that I don't have to look like, act like, sound like, preach like, and teach like anyone else besides myself. I am great at being me. I no longer live my life for what others think I should be. I am simply who God designed me to be. Yes, there are days when I have no idea who that is, but the journey to discovering her is one that I have learned to embrace and enjoy.

I embrace the fact that I don't have to be what I saw in church growing up because I am the church. I can listen to the Mississippi Mass choir or Nicki Minaj; I feel God everywhere. The church lives inside of me and what I show up as. I am conscious of the startling fact that I may be the only expression of God that someone gets to see, so I'm learning to tread wisely and just be me. I am comfortable in knowing that God is not on a pedestal where I can't reach, but lives within me, reflects me, uses me when needed and loves me enough to provide me with nothing but the best. I trust God, and that feels real to me. I encourage you to give yourself permission to be YOU, and be good at it! There is no one else on the face of this earth that can do you better than you!

With Love,
Ms. Mahogany

FOR DERRICK: Don't Throw in the Towel!
Rev. Dr. L. Christi Hunter
New York, NY

"Oh I Give Up!"

How many times have you felt like throwing in the towel on God? Life just hasn't been easy, kind, fair, or moving in the direction you believe it should. How often have you asked the questions, "GOD WHERE ARE YOU?" "CAN YOU HEAR ME?" "ARE YOU THERE GOD? IT'S (your name here)!"? Only to get silence from you know, God the Father, who promises to never leave or forsake you?

 I have a friend who recently posted on Facebook that he was on the brink of giving up. This is what he wrote:

"FB family here's hoping someone can offer some constructive advice, pearls of wisdom, something I can use. Today I received some extremely disappointing news, which has left me at a crossroads, unsure of what the rest of my life holds. Roughly three years ago at the apex of my health crisis a friend of mine told me, as I was trying to wrap my mind around leaving my life as I knew it, my home, my security, my independence, my manhood behind, that God sometimes has to remove things in our lives to make room for new blessings that He has for us. Well I'm sad to say I have yet to see restoration and I wonder just how much more of my life must I surrender? I have never felt more deflated and unsure of just what my future life holds. I don't know what to do, where to turn or even what to pray for anymore because I'm not sure that God is even listening. I will say that the usual "be encouraged, just pray etc.",

none of that is going to assuage my anxiety. I just feel that there has to be more to this thing called life than simply existing and what a poor existence it is!

I love this friend more than words can express. I feel his pain because I have walked several miles in his shoes. I fully understand where he is, how frustrated he is, how abandoned by God he feels, and just how ready he is to give up on EVERYTHING, especially God. How do I offer comfort? What words of encouragement can I share to help my brother and friend get beyond throwing in the towel, giving up on his journey and giving up on God?

One thing that resonates for me is the question that my friend asks – "How much more of my life must I surrender?" Well beloved, this life isn't yours, belongs to God! You must surrender all, your will must be lost in His. Perhaps this journey isn't for you; maybe someone is watching you and your struggle. What if God is using you to get someone's attention? Your response is KEY! Not only is the lesson for those of us whose lives you touch, your mother, siblings, church family, it is for the stranger who admires you from a distance…heck IT IS FOR ME!!!

We don't want the people we love to feel pain. We don't want them to face difficulty, sadness or hard times and when they do, we want to soothe their soul. We want life to be the fairytale we imagine it to be. However, life rarely falls in line with our plans unless that plan is in direct alignment with what God has outlined, and even then we will have to walk a rocky road. Why you might ask? Well, I believe God will allow difficult times so that we can and will come to the end of ourselves and to the beginning of HIM! We must do just what the word charges… *"Trust in the Lord with all your heart and lean not on your own understanding; in all your ways submit to Him, and He will make your paths straight."* (Proverbs 3:5-6 NIV). This is so much easier said than done.

In trusting, one must let go - let go of fear, uncertainty and control. How? You must be willing to be vulnerable, you have to be ok with the unknown, but most of all, you must be able to live in, and with, the silence. You must KNOW beyond all question that if we remain *"…steadfast, immovable, always abounding in the work of the Lord…your labor is not in vain."* (1 Cor. 15:58 ESV). The promise of God is He will ALWAYS work it out, but He requires something from us – *"Faint not"* (Luke 18:1), *"Be steadfast"* (1 Cor. 15:58), *"Don't grow weary in well doing."* (Gal. 6:9). God will do His part if we do our part! Perhaps it is time to consider getting back to basics. Maybe going back to the beginning will cause this bump in the road to become a little less difficult to travel. This may be a lot easier said than done! After all I am suggesting that you look at your relationship with God and consider reconnecting on a different level.

Beloved friend of mine, I love you, and a real friend will speak the truth in love. It is time for you to get back to basics!!! The Bible has the answer! The answer that works for me is found in 2 Chronicles 7:14. *"If my people, who are called by my name, will humble themselves and pray and seek my face and turn from their wicked ways, then will I hear from heaven and will forgive their sin and will restore their land."*

Let's take an up close look at this verse -

"If" is a conjunction, the state of which one must work in combination with, so, we must work with God. *"My people..."* YOU MUST ACKNOWLEDGE THAT YOU BELONG TO GOD. *"Who are called by MY name..."* the world also acknowledges who you are and whose you are. *"Will humble..."* (become meek, unassuming, submissive, modest, respectful, lower, reserved, CONTENT with) *"themselves and pray..."* It isn't about you talk to God! Stop focusing on you and your needs, wants, desire and focus on what the Lord has to say. *"And seek..."* (Follow, explore, hunt down, pursue and chase after) *"My face..."* Ask the question... what does God want (not what do I want)? Now the hard work comes in! You must do something – *"and turn..."* (Bend, bow, change) *"from their wicked* (contemptible, degenerate, depraved, devilish, egregious, evil, fiendish, flagitious, foul, gross, guilty, heartless, heinous, immoral, impious, impish, incorrigible, indecent, irreligious, low-down, mean, nasty, naughty, nefarious, profane, rotten scandalous, shameful, shameless, sinful, unethical, unprincipled, unrighteous, vicious, vile, villainous, wayward, worthless) *ways..."* After you have done all of this, God will do HIS part! He will hear us, He will forgive us (for being a hot mess), and most of all God WILL RESTORE US. Not to what we use to be but, the restoration will be what God wants us to be - bigger, better, and brighter than what we could have ever imagined or hoped for!

Lord how blessed we are by You and because of You! Thank you for the standard that moves us to a place and space where we can and long to meet with You daily.

SCARED OUTTA BEING A LESBIAN
Ferrin Mitchell
Toledo, OH

One judicious morning

Wakened by a bad dream.

Parallel to myself, but a new and better being.

My closet had been swept clean.

Ironically conscious and accepting

Of this refreshing self-admission

That I was in fact a L...L...L.

I had been scared out of being a lesbian!

I rejected the label!

All the negative connotations.

Like if I was, I had to hate men.

But that's a sad myth,

Such misguided ignorance.

Well if that's not it then

Your Dad must have been abusive

Or probably just absent.

Though our relationship isn't perfect,

Honestly, I have no "Daddy complex."

He wasn't just present, he was there.

Sometimes he even did my hair.

So what is it then?

Were you raped by some pig,

Or molested by some bigot?

Nope, that's not even it.

Check "None of the above."

And from where I'm sitting

It's a blessing from Above.

Because it takes courage to divulge.

To risk losing the ones you love.

To face such heavy opposition,

At The Table

From education to religion,

From strangers to kin.

How you go from just a basketball player

To a hell bound abomination.

All such naive contentions.

So let me state my position;

It's all a transition.

From the little girl I was then,

To the woman I'm becoming now.

Strong and Proud.

I'll even shout it out loud,

Never be a coward again.

And never let myself be scared out of being a Lesbian.

DEATH OF A BLACK GOD:
Confronting the Issue of Gays in the Black Church
Isis Pickens
Los Angeles, CA

She came into the office, asking for something simple, bottled water, a pen or napkin of some sort. The details of her request escape me three years later. I remember only the look on her grandmother's face when, a fellow basketball player referred to her by the wrong gender. "Hey, tell him we got room for one more player, if he wants to get in on a game," he said. Her eyes were frozen; terrified that someone had called her masculine baby girl a 'him' in front of the Pastor's wife. I politely ignored his mistake in the way good Christian women do, and informed her that a position had opened up on the court down the hall. From there we developed a mentor- mentee relationship, with me writing college recommendation letters and putting in a first lady call for her first ever pay check job.

Things went on this way until we received a personal invitation to a champagne party for prom; our sixth that year. We arrived late, card in hand. We waited with a small crowd of aunties, cousins, friends and grandma of course, to get a glimpse of the star in her prom best. She emerged from the bathroom, dressed very dapper in a three piece suit, equipped with an expensive tie, black wing-tip shoes and a big face watch. She asked for a picture with the Pastor and First Lady. Her grandmother held her breath. "Get in the middle," my husband says.

"You look great." I add. Smile. Flash. "Thank you." We wave, as the shiny custom Buick pulls off down the street. We thank the host, say our good byes. "Thank you so much for coming," her grandmother says. "Of course, we don't pass up free food," I joke, not really sure of what else to say and turn toward the car. I did not see her stretched arms, until they were wrapped around my neck. "Thank you," she says again, with a bit more power. "I mean it. Thanks for everything. Thank you for loving my baby. I don't know nothing about how she's living. I don't know about them things. All I know is when I'm hurt, she's the one who rubs my feet. When I need medicine, she's the one who goes and gets it. Thank you for loving us. We left the last church because the First Lady just wanted to hurt my baby and she's just a kid, you know? She's a good kid." "She is," I say. We are both crying. Until that moment, our connection mirrored the long unspoken relationship homosexuality has had with the black church.

My husband and I discuss the intense exchange in the car. I am visibly angered by the things her grandmother said the first lady did to my mentee. This is not an unfamiliar dilemma for us. Having been raised in a black Baptist church and now as new leaders of one, we are familiar with resistance to the idea of acceptance. The recent harsh and ungodly hate some of our church members have endured because of their sexual orientation is beginning to weigh on my spirit. "I'm afraid that I am losing my religion." I confess.

Our stance is clear and firm. "All have access to God's love." We believe this with every breath in us. This belief has contributed to our success as spiritual leaders in Los Angeles. In three short years we have seen congregational growth at a rate of 300%. We have hosted national scholars and political figures, spearheaded an international mission trip to Brazil and started a community garden, still we face great uncertainty due to the human limitations of love so unfortunately prevalent in black churches.

Recently, a wonderful woman came and started a much needed youth and fitness program at the church. She loved the word that God had given my husband and enjoyed the change happening in her life so much, she joined! Then, she introduced us to her girlfriend of eight years. They asked for counseling. Believing firmly that God is love and all have access to that love, we agreed. We found them to have a rock solid love of God and one another. The commitment and compromise they shared was astounding, even down to the raising of their child. They asked that my husband perform a civil union ceremony, (as of this writing California has not legalized gay marriage or as a comedian once said, marriage.). Being very big on marriage, he agreed. I have said we believe God is love right? In any and every form, God is love and that does not have conditions. They scheduled the ceremony for February of 2013, booked a location two cities away and we quietly planned without informing the church.

We were first shocked when the couple asked a month from the scheduled date to have the ceremony take place in the sanctuary, among their church family. My husband and I prayed and agreed. It was the right thing to do. In the process of getting things together, my husband came across the deacon board; the good old Baptist deacon board. They put an immediate stop to the plans. They would have none of it. They began opposing everything he did thereafter.

Again we went to prayer. We decided to move forward with sharing God's love with anyone who asked for it. My husband confessed to me that although scared, he could not believe and preach about God's love if he was unable to live it.

Because we believe in equality, because we believe that everyone has access to God's love, we have of course been labeled as gay. We have heard the rumors swirling the pews about our "arrangement". The unprecedented suspension comes, in the form of a letter from the deacon board, amid the opposition of the congregation. My husband's pay is cut. I am nervous because we have children and bills. Of course, being of strong faith, I do believe God will provide. He confides in me that this move may very well end his job as Pastor of the church and I am a instantly frustrated with LA, black folks and black Christianity. The matter has upset me, and I confess to him, that "I am losing my religion."

He admits to his own fears, but assures me the actions of the members and my mentee's former spiritual leaders are merely homophobic. But, I am very leery of using the term "homophobia" in connection with the black church. I am not sure that the term or its meaning applies to black Christianity. The black church has always had a relationship with the LGBT community. Although the black church has come out openly against same sex marriage and homosexual lifestyle(s), gays have had a profound effect on the ways in which black church is performed and ultimately experienced. One can even argue that black gay male identity has made a mark on the sound of black gospel music, which is a focal point of worship in the black church. If homophobia is the fear of homosexuals, I would say that it does not belong in conversation with the black church. The long standing history of co-existing and equal participation in worship is documented in our church narratives and our art, as proven by the presence of homosexual culture in our artistic representations and reproductions of black church in popular culture (note: the gay choir director, or the overly excited worshipper and the religious gay hairdresser, who quotes scriptures as he curls hair. The black church as a culture-maker, does not have a fear of homosexuals. What we have, is a lack of respect for them.

As articulated by my mentee's dear grandmother, the issue of homosexuality in the black church is problematic for reasons beyond theological differences. As a spiritual entity, the black church's duty is to bridge any and all connections to God. As humans (black or otherwise), we experience God essentially two ways: Private and Communal. The black church's stance on homosexuality is increasingly troubling for gay black Christians fundamentally due to the human principle of communal faith. A large part of black cultural identity is based on how we experience spirituality. Part of being black in America (and possibly everywhere else) is spirituality; a majority of our spiritual experiences are tied to each other.

 I am alarmed at the spiritual disrespect of our gay and lesbian brothers and sisters, because of the potentially harmful role it may play in the destruction of their spiritual identities. As a spiritual leader I do not want to hold the knife that severs someone's connection to God. By rejecting them, we are in fact killing their identity and this has a genuine effect on their spirituality. They now have one less way to experience God. As human beings we don't live separate from one another. We know and understand love through interaction with each other. When we do not acknowledge the complete identity of our gay brothers and sisters, we are robbing them and ourselves of more opportunities to love and experience God.

I think at its core, the issue of homosexuality in the black church is an issue of self-righteousness. Black Christian identity has wrapped itself in the robe of moral authority. I am thinking of Rev. Dr. Martin Luther King, Jr., Harriet 'Moses' Tubman and the long list of mega church pastors who have defended the rights of poor single women. Much of our spiritual platform revolves around the parallels between Jesus' persecution and the persecution of blacks in the Americas. This comparison has allowed us to fully embrace Christianity in ways that other colonized and religiously oppressed groups have not. This has also given us a religious license to a sort of cultural blamelessness. We have 'moral authority' on our side. We have gained spiritual collateral, recognized as valuable beyond our racial marginalization. Black faith is called upon by troubled white leaders, our spiritual music is needed to sooth the ills of human tragedy and our theology has become the slogan for other movements across the globe.

When white churches or other faith based groups lean toward an 'open' or 'affirming' position on gays in the church, unlike other aspects of black culture, we do not follow. This is because, unlike politics and education, blacks do not feel inferior to whites in spirituality. We have been justified in Jesus. We embrace, even flaunt our spiritual authority. So much so, that our (the black church's) music, social triumphs and public adoration cannot absorb critique. It is the one trait that has helped us as a people overcome unspeakable tragedies. Unfortunately, it is also the same trait that threatens to destroy the future of the black church.

The black church sees no need for spiritual growth, because history has told us that we've gotten it right. Our faith helped us endure and overcome slavery. It was the catalyst for our rise out of segregation and the platform for many of our political leaders. This perverted sense of moral authority, is prohibiting us from taking a sincere look at ourselves and the state of our church. Oh but the dangers that lie ahead! The damage in maintaining our current stance on this subject reaches far beyond the dismantling of the black church. It pierces much deeper into the depths of our very being, and so begins the disintegration of our souls. The point where something stops growing is simultaneously the point in which it starts dying. I am a witness to this death. In my ministry, I hear the silent tears of mothers, fathers and friends. People are dying literally, dying to know God. They are killing themselves with drugs, sex and spiritual numbness, because we are too religious to tell them, that they are made perfect in God, just as they are.

I don't consider myself an expert on the matter. Nor do I have the magic remedy for calming the storm that is fast arising within us. I know only that I've been called to stand in the gap for those who lacked spiritual confidence before, and I once again find myself on bended knee.

YOU ARE NOT CONDEMNED!

"Therefore there is now no condemnation for those who are in Christ Jesus. For the law of the Spirit of life in Christ Jesus has set you free from the law of sin and of death...."

Romans 8:1-2

OUT ON A "W.I.M."

Rev. Leslie Oliver
Charlotte, NC

I had to participate in "scripture showers" as a preacher's kid, where you were required to recite scripture on demand. Someone always beat me to "Jesus wept" (the shortest verse in the bible), so I'd recite the 23rd Psalm. I had no idea that I'd live that powerful word several times over later in my youth and my adulthood. Many nights, while enduring the stinging lashes of sexual abuse and witnessing the acid rain of domestic violence, I'd recite this powerful collection of verses, curled up in a ball in dark corners or under worn mattresses. The shadows of death appeared like lightning to me, a child, the assuming and consummate model of God's pure love.

The pain of my formative years convinced me that God had forgotten me, and I spent most of my twenties chasing the wind of death and destruction, murmuring "Woe is me" (W.I.M.) every chance I could. It was God's fault that I was cursed and left with fear, mistrust and apathy. I was sure that my narrative was completed. As God would ordain it, grace, mercy, maturity and motherhood all ganged up on me in my thirties to offer me a new perspective on the rollercoaster ride that had become my journey and my emotional crutch. In my forties, I landed right back onto the 23rd Psalm, my loyal weaponry and war cry, which revealed itself to me anew and showed me how to respond to fear and its extensions rather than react to them.

As I noticed how my life and purpose were improving, I began proclaiming "Whoa! It's me!" (W.I.M.) everywhere someone would listen. I affirmed myself as a chosen vessel for God and declared a new understanding of the presence and power of God in my life, just as King David had done in this transformative text.

What made David such a great man was not his accomplishments or accrued wealth, but his acknowledgment of a greater power and purpose in good and bad times. He had moments where he reacted, but most of his moments were responses, positive reactions to his circumstances. As humans in the 21st century, we are taught to react negatively to things that happen. It's a set up from the get up. Our posture in the universe will inform how and when we "go out on a W.I.M." to declare the power of God in our ever-changing lives. The key to achieving higher levels of favor is to follow the example of King David, and unapologetically affirm that you are loved and cared for.

Consider each situation of your life as an honor. Resist reactions and embrace responses. Shift your perspective, your W.I.M. from the "woe is me" to the "Whoa! It's me!". It's you that is renewed! It's you that is elevated, healed, transformed, perfected. Then wait and watch for God to show you miracles worth shouting about. With every blessing, new mercy and breakthrough, go "OUT

ON A W.I.M." and declare the power and presence of God with new understanding. Your self-affirmation, even in rough times, will become infectious, and by seeing the light in your life, others will be inspired to go out on a "W.I.M." with you.

ONE BLADE OF HIGH GRASS

Cole Thomas
Atlanta, GA

If you knew you could neither fail nor succeed

That you're never truly adverse or agreed

That sometimes you're the bloom and sometimes the seed

Would it affect the way you see others?

If you someday learned you're the sky, not the plane

Or the ones you despise aren't pollution, but wings

That you're set like a rock-circled bonfire in spring

Would you embrace your mothers and brothers?

If you could receive sentiments you express

"You're heroic." "You're sensual. "Fool!" "You're a mess."

When we reach for that collective personal best

Will that silence our curses and jeers?

At The Table

Who among us would even give up one half?

Become sunlight or shade on someone's hazy path?

What if we ARE that someone and neighbors just
laughed?

Would we build faith or in bitterness die?

What if you felt so wholly helpless at night

Afraid nothing you'll ever become will be right?

Add to that the belief you walk in your own might

Then, imagine the terror, the hell.

We're each a speck

on the tip

of one blade

of high grass

Yet empowered, programmed to impact and to last

To be fostered, to foster lessons from our past

Across genders, affinities, language or class.

Let's acknowledge we can neither fail nor succeed

Let's admit we're not fully adverse or agreed

Cultivate harmony whether blossom or seed

Circumspectly about our lives go.

Silences

Sit quietly and imagine the intersections human perception, decision-making, judgment and values. Seek to comprehend silences- yours and others'. We think we know exactly how we would respond to a difficult dilemma so long as we never actually have to face it. We believe that we know ourselves intimately, and yet what we know is limited by those things we have yet to experience and by those things God has yet to reveal to us.

Our default, our kneejerk response is to judge and dismiss those who make decisions that seem to defy reason.

Perhaps it is merely human nature to do so. Remember, someone somewhere feels that you, too, are ludicrous in your beliefs, values, judgment, conclusions and actions. Recognize this, since intentionally considering and extenuating another person's circumstances can detour us from the deceptively smooth path of self-righteous indignation. You see, that pot-o-gold at the path's end is filled with humble pie, and like fruit cake, it makes an impression!

So much of how we approach our everyday lives is conditional, contextual, and relative. It is a great challenge to simultaneously explore widely and yet keep clear boundaries; to forgive without becoming a target; and to be open yet vigilant. This precarious balance, it turns out, rides in on the shoulders of wisdom, sliding almost undetected, into the pockets of those of us with the pie-covered chins.

TO THE ENDS OF THE EARTH:
Reading the Ethiopian Eunuch in Acts 8 through a Contemporary Lens
Asher Kolieboi
Nashville, TN

Traditional interpretations of scripture have significantly marginalized the voices of those who live at the edges of society. But the growing fields of queer biblical studies and racial/ethnic critique have created discourses that not only explore queer and of color characters within the Bible but also seek to create a theology that affirms sexual and racial minorities. Both these ideological criticisms are influenced by the existence of critical race and gender theory throughout the academy as well as queer liberation and racial justice social movements. Queer biblical criticism and racial/ethnic criticism utilize an optic connected to the struggle of the communities from which they emerged. Here I explore the conversion of the Ethiopian eunuch in Acts 8:26-40 as a biblical story affirming queer of color bodies. Through a queer of color reading of the eunuch in Acts 8, I argue that the eunuch is a dynamic and ambiguous character that can be seen as liberating to my lesbian, gay, bisexual, transgender siblings of color. The eunuch serves as a model for queer and transgender people of color who are silenced, condemned, and demonized by society and the church.

Historically queer has been used as a derogatory term for lesbian, gay, bisexual, transgender, and queer people. But in the last few decades many in the community have reclaimed the term as both an umbrella term and a word that represents anything that is radically different from what society deems normal. Queer theory incorporates the negative connotations of traditional understanding of queer and uses this to critique sociocultural constructs of gender, race, sex, and class. Thus, to use queer as a verb means to challenge and resist the established concepts of the norm. This subversion allows for liberation from systems of stratification and domination that demarcate "normal" from "abnormal."

Traditional gender and queer theorists have failed to recognize the importance of race and class to queer experiences, limiting their analysis to gender and sexuality. But the works of queer scholars of color and scholars of color who integrate queer identities into their work (including Audre Lorde and Gloria Anzaldua in women's studies and Tat-siong Benny Liew and Patrick Cheng in biblical studies) take traditional queer scholarship's singular focus to task. They, and I, argue that to truly queer a subject means seeing the complexity of identity through an intersectional lens that resists the inclination to view anything in a narrow or singular scope. Thus, a study of Acts 8:26-40 through a queer of color lens means viewing the eunuch as a multilevel character constructed by the authors of Luke Acts as such.

The story of the Ethiopian eunuch is the story of a body that is dehumanized for refusing classification and is nonetheless accepted into the body of Christ without compromise.

The Ethiopian eunuch in Acts 8:26-40 functions as a queer narrative because the eunuch as a character embodies an ambiguous identity that exists at the margins of social life. The eunuch, and what he represents, falls outside of culturally constructed norms, destabilizing fixed categories of gender, race, and class. Simultaneously embodying shame/righteousness and impurity/purity, the eunuch's identities are a deliberate inclusion on the part of the narrator to illustrate that anyone can be a follower of Christ.

The Ethiopian eunuch is the first person to be converted to Christianity in the New Testament. This is not a mere coincidence but a purposeful inclusion. Similar to other converts in Luke and Acts, the eunuch occupies a complex or queer position in antiquity. Other Lucan parables place a significant amount of attention on those who occupy the lowest rung of social life. This includes a tax collector (Luke 19:1-10), a widow (Luke 21-22), and a man riddled with disease (Acts 28:7-10).

The character is identified first as an Ethiopian, a word that denotes his place of origin and race. Little was known about Ethiopia in the ancient world. As a black person, the eunuch evokes Greco-Roman stereotypes about blackness and its equation with evil and immorality.

This inclusion was intentional on the part of the authors who knew the cultural connotations that arose with the use of "Ethiopian" as a descriptor.

The eunuch is only identified once in the passage as Ethiopian. The other four times he is simply called eunouchos or eunuch (vs. 34, 36, 38, 39). The emphasis on the character's gender could be an attempt to draw upon cultural codes and identity markers of the gender ambiguous eunuch. In Greco-Roman culture, masculinity was comprised of a complex matrix of identity that was informed by a person's social status, sexuality, and gender. Masculinity was contingent upon the ability to "dominate unmen-women, foreigners, slaves, and children."[1] So in addition to not having a penis and failing to accord with physical ideals of maleness, the eunuch could not successfully recreate socially prescribed notions of maleness and masculinity. The eunuch's inability to present and perform the type of masculinity expected in antiquity meant his very existence challenged the definition of man or male in a society that relied heavily on gender classification.

This queering of masculinity made eunuchs and their bodies the subject of disdain. Feminine in appearance and unable to procreate, the eunuch embodied queerness. Second-century satirist Lucian of Samosata narrates a tale of a eunuch whose nemesis describes him saying, "Markedly smooth of jowl (beardless) and effeminate in voice, a eunuch was an ambiguous sort of

---

[1] Burke, *Queering Early Christian Discourse: The Ethiopian Eunuch*, 175

creature like a crow, which cannot be reckoned either with doves or with ravens."2 Neither man nor woman, the unclassifiable body of the eunuch was often positioned as unnatural, unclean, and unholy.

Numerous biblical scriptures in the Hebrew Bible reflect the cultural undesirability of the eunuch. Leviticus 21-20 lists them among those who "shall not come near to offer the food of his God" (Leviticus 21-20 NRSV). Similarly, Deuteronomy excludes eunuchs from worshiping in the temple: "No one whose testicles are crushed or whose penis is cut off shall be admitted to the assembly of the Lord" (Deuteronomy 23:1 NRSV). The purity laws at the time were well known to the authors and readers of Luke Acts, providing a subtext to the passage in Acts 8; this could allow for a deeper interpretation of the eunuch's experience as a devout queer person of faith in a culture that marked him as impure.

Due to customary laws, the eunuch in Acts 8:26-40 may not have been allowed in the temple. While the passage states that he "had come to Jerusalem to worship" (Acts 8:27 NRSV), there is no confirmation that he was received or allowed to worship in the temple. Despite his vocation and status in Ethiopia in the queen's court, the eunuch may have been turned away. As a black queer or transman whose very existence embodied a challenge to

---

[2] Quoted in Spencer, *The Ethiopian Eunuch and His Bible: A Social-Science Analysis,* 157

traditional social roles in antiquity, he could have been refused admission in to the temple despite his piety and devotion.

After the crucifixion of Jesus, criticism of the temple was a common narrative theme raised by the authors of Luke Acts. Unwelcoming to outsiders, the temple had become exploitative, only "serving the political interests of the opportunistic high-priestly party and shutting out all but those know to be ritually pure."3 Phillip's willingness to explain the text and proclaim the good news about Jesus to the eunuch (Acts 8:35) is therefore not a minor event. It is a message to those denied by the church and society that they are included in the good news.

The story of the Ethiopian eunuch is a story of liberation for those working against white heterosexist understandings of Christianity. This ambiguous queer outsider is the first official convert to Christianity in the Bible, and his conversion and baptism send a message to those condemned by the church: the gospel is meant to be welcoming to all. Lesbian, gay, bisexual, transgender, and queer Christians, especially those of color who struggle to keep faith when they are denied by the church and shunned by society for failing to reproduce traditional notions of gender and sexuality, can draw their inspiration from this humble servant in Acts. Demonized and condemned by our faith communities "we have struggled to make sense of scripture, to find our place in it, when others would use it to

---

[3] Spencer, *The Ethiopian Eunuch and His Bible: A Social-Science Analysis*, 160

condemn us."4 Like the eunuch, our complex identities challenge a world built on uniformity that punishes those with ambiguous and shifting identities. Acts 8:26-40 is a reminder to gender and sexual minorities that we must seek to create church and community outside of the established church. Like the eunuch we may travel from the ends of the earth to find community and refuge but be turned away by a church that has forgotten its purpose. But also like him, we must find a new community that embraces all.

Work Cited

- Burke , Sean . "Queering Early Christian Discourse: The Ethiopian Eunuch." *Bible trouble queer reading at the boundaries of biblical scholarship.* Atlanta: Society of Biblical Literature, 2011. 175-190. Print.

- West, Mona . "The Story of the Ethiopian Eunuch." *The queer Bible commentary.* London: SCM, 2006. 573-574. Print.

- Scott, Spencer. "The Ethiopian Eunuch and His Bible: a Social-Science Analysis" Paul's Odyssey in Acts: Status Struggles and Island Adventures Biblical Theology Bulletin: A Journal of Bible and Theology November 1, 1998 28: 150-159

---

4 West, *Queer Bible commentary*, 573

EXPOSED BY A PROPHET
A Devotional
Rev. E. Taylor Doctor
Atlanta, GA

2 Samuel 12:1-7; 13 (NRSV):
"¹and the LORD sent Nathan to David. He came to him, and said to him, "There were two men in a certain city, the one rich and the other poor. ²The rich man had very many flocks and herds; ³but the poor man had nothing but one little ewe lamb, which he had bought. He brought it up, and it grew up with him and with his children; it used to eat of his meager fare, and drink from his cup, and lie in his bosom, and it was like a daughter to him. ⁴Now there came a traveler to the rich man, and he was loath to take one of his own flock or herd to prepare for the wayfarer who had come to him, but he took the poor man's lamb, and prepared that for the guest who had come to him." ⁵Then David's anger was greatly kindled against the man. He said to Nathan, "As the LORD lives, the man who has done this deserves to die; ⁶he shall restore the lamb fourfold, because he did this thing, and because he had no pity." ⁷Nathan said to David, "You are the man! Thus says the LORD, the God of Israel: I anointed you king over Israel, and I rescued you from the hand of Saul; ¹³David said to Nathan, "I have sinned against the LORD." Nathan said to David, "Now the LORD has put away your sin; you shall not die."

The story behind this devotional is paralleled with experiences from my past, specifically my coming out journey. It was a journey that prompted me to examine myself with the utmost scrutiny. After completely accepting my call to preach the gospel around age 17 (though I recall my initial call some 5 years earlier), I found myself in various situations that caused me to reevaluate myself, my actions, my words and even my thinking. As the adage says, "You better check yourself, before you wreck yourself." I was a college student doing well in my degree program and serving in various capacities at church and things started to happen that were almost life altering; like that car accident on Interstate 95 in Richmond, Virginia where I resided that made me see white light or that now questionable choice of leaving my family church to join another church only to be as I look back on it now, overlooked in ministry again. It happens to all of us in life at times. We find ourselves pushing so hard for acceptance and approval of others that we allow the words we speak to be contradictory, the actions we take to be life threatening, and the thoughts we have to be self-degrading.

I moved to Atlanta Georgia on August 20, 2012 and I found myself a first semester, first year seminary student at the Interdenominational Theological Center and in metaphor, I was a closet full of skeletons, situations and experiences. Encounters that I had stored away in the recesses of my conscience and the closet was now so full that if I did not stand in front of the door all of me would have come spilling out and I would have been bleeding EVERYWHERE. All of us do not have a testimony alike to David; but all of us do have one. The beauty of David's life and ministry is that though David was not perfect, David was repentant and that is what made David a man after G-d's own heart. David's sin was what he did with Bathsheba and Uriah; your sin or my sin might be what we do not do. Our sin may be sitting on the gifts and graces that G-d has given us; the sin comes then when we live in denial of those things that G-d has called each of us to. Thus, the greatest sin is not being true to yourself. G-d did not call any of us for who you are; G-d called us for who G-d wants us to be. The conscience of who we are is too often shoved into the closet because it/they will expose us to who we really are. It will confront us, convict us and correct us.

Looking into the text, Nathan appears in this text as a prophet to David or in other words a conscience for David. The job of a prophet is to speak truth to light, thus often times exposing us for who we really are. Nathan shares with David the story about a rich man who steals the only ewe lamb that a poor man owns. David does not realize that Nathan is referring to him until later in the text and even kindles anger toward the story's main character. Nathan's response to David's anger is timely. In the very next verse Nathan says to David "YOU ARE THE MAN!"

Nathan comes first as a conscience confrontation (verses 1-4) to David. Nathan offers constructive criticism unto David. He made it plain so that David cannot be confused about any part of the occurrence. Nathan also serves as David's conviction (verses 5-6). Because David is charged with the care of the House of Israel (or rather the people of G-d), the conscience confrontation now comes to convict him about his actions, for how can David care for the people with complexities all around him?

David's fear of dealing with who he really is comes because he knows that in dealing with the mirror, EVERYTHING will have to change. You know the saying, "If you do what you have always done, you get the same results." However if we make conscious efforts to change things for the better we will find ourselves in different places with new graces from G-d. The truth of this text is that like David, I can live through the hell I have created. Being introspective must be foundational if G-d will be able to use us for effective ministry.

Nathan comes to confront, convict and also to offer correction (verse 13) to David. The correction is simple - repent and you shall live. And so we see David utter these words, "*I have sinned against the Lord.*" Nathan then offers the reassurance that we all need to hear at various times in life when he says, "*Now the Lord has put away your sin; you shall not die.*" At the end of the day, the door to accountability must be opened and personal examination must take place. Nathan here serves as David's conscience and forces David to begin to deal with those things in the closet that would have continued haunting him. So it is with each of us. It is imperative that we recognize the person or persons who are sent to serve as our conscience confrontation, conviction and correction. These people will always confront us in love and complete honesty. They will show up in all areas of our lives to make sure we are living and being our maximum potential. They will help us to understand that we cannot carry old baggage into new situations. They will tell us to get rid of the drama! They will be our mirror and our conscience. This will cause us to do proclaim as David did in his expression of evolving liberation in Psalm 51:10-12: *"Create in me a pure heart, O God, and renew a steadfast spirit within me. Do not cast me from your presence or take your Holy Spirit from me. Restore to me the joy of your salvation and grant me a willing spirit, to sustain me..."*

This devotional is dedicated to my Nathans: My immediate family, Dr. Lisa M. Allen, Rev. Brittany Powell, Rev. Renetta Hobson, Overseer Yvonne M. Harrision, Apostle David B. Lay, Dr. Ronald E. Peters and Dr. F. Keith Slaughter. Each of you have participated intricately in specific seasons of my journey and each moment spent with you reminds me that G-d has called me for greatness. You are my spiritual sages.

TRANSITION//TRANSFORMATION
Stephfon Guidry
New York, NY

God working on you

Wrapping you

Cocoon

Pain, temptation

Hurt

Nights spent crying yourself to sleep

The only arms you felt were your own

Forget the flesh

The Holy Spirit was there

God was there

Jesus' blood was running to and through you

In the womb

In your cocoon

As your praise raised you on to a branch

At The Table

You grabbed and held on for dear life

You knew the battle

Made you weary

You needed a moment

A second to stop the fight

God gave you the cocoon

The Armor in his word

So no predator no snake no bird

Could touch you in your cocoon

You were wrapped up

By design

You changed from

A fuzzy crawling

Caterpillar

A baby an infant

In for the faith filled trip

Remember Calvary

It is your branch

Remember the cross it

Is your tree

Remember the 3 days

Your savior rose

He rose

Feel the Cocoon

Hardening

It's blocking out those that

Criticize your peculiar nature

Your change

Your manifestation of Gods new

RENEWED creation in you

Seasons change

Time passes

People lose interest in you

But the Cocoon is so strong

At The Table

You are unbothered

You are not alone

Angels are guarding your transition

Soon day breaks

Sun hits your shell

It shakes

It shifts

Its uneasy it may even be un pleasant

At first to be in this new body

Your eyes aren't open

All you can see now is the darkness of the cocoon

You think it is a trap

A prison

Now

God has not left you

God is there he is there in the darkness

It is God's will

The Spirit the Holy Ghost rockin' the Cocoon

Telling you it is time

A crack in the shell and the light shimmers through

You smell the sweet honey

The nectar of God's love

All of a sudden

In a Blinding flash

You open your wings

OPEN YOUR WINGS

Open yourself

Eyes are open

A being changed

Transformed

Infused with a new spirit

A raw transitioning

You can't Go back

Because a buttafly is not a caterpillar

At The Table

Let your wings show the struggle

There is beauty in your tears

Let your eyes show the joy

There is praise in your tears

Fly up Fly down

All around the mountain

Lay your feet on

The new consecrated ground

A new spirit in the Lord

Amen ashe Amen

YOU ARE GOD'S MASTERPIECE!

"For we are God's masterpiece. He has created us anew in Christ Jesus, so we can do the good things he planned for us long ago."
Ephesians 2:10

HE KNOWS ME
Min. Janet Lafontaine
Bronx, NY

Jeremiah 1:4-9

4 Now the word of the LORD came to me, saying,
5 "Before I formed you in the womb I knew you,
and before you were born I consecrated you;
I appointed you a prophet to the nations."
6 Then I said, "Ah, Lord GOD! Behold, I do not know how to
speak, for I am only a youth." 7 But the LORD said to me,
"Do not say, 'I am only a youth'
for to all to whom I send you, you shall go,
and whatever I command you, you shall speak.
8 Do not be afraid of them,
for I am with you to deliver you,
declares the LORD."
9 Then the LORD put out his hand and touched my mouth. And
the LORD said to me,
"Behold, I have put my words in your mouth."

I read these words and realized that the Lord really DOES know me. He knew who I would be before I did. He knows what I will become even though I don't fully know. He sees things in me that I never dreamed I would. He knew me in all my complexities, because He made them all, in His image.

It wasn't too long ago that I had this epiphany. There was a time when I didn't know why I was alive and what purpose I would serve. I often wondered why God would allow me to be who I am knowing that I would be ostracized, ridiculed, discriminated against, made fun of, talked about, oppressed, and dare I say, damned to hell. WHY LORD? WHY? I would ask. His answer was always the same, "Why NOT you? Why can't I call you? Why can't I use you?"

Let me be clear; I am a woman of color. I am saved. I have been called to ministry. I am a musician. I am also a lesbian. In today's society, many of those things do not mix. Traditional churches say that I cannot be gay and saved, that I cannot be a woman and called to ministry. That I'm supposed to sit quietly, never be open about who I am, never be transparent, because I will bring shame to the church. Like a fool, I believed that for a long time. For years I didn't speak of my orientation. I kept my business just that, my business. I went to church, played my instrument and went home. I didn't make a lot of friends (especially female friends) because I had to hear rumors. I knew people were whispering about me. They wanted to know how I rolled but dared not ask me. Don't even get me started about the sermons I would have to sit through, where their base scriptures would be Leviticus, or Romans, or the story of Sodom and Gomorrah.

At the age of fourteen I developed my first crush on a girl who would later become a dear friend. It was 1989 and I was a freshman in high school in California. I had no idea at the time what exactly I was feeling; all I knew was that I thought she was beautiful; her shape, the way she talked to me, the way she danced…it fascinated me to no end. But, there was a problem: I was fourteen, saved, and wasn't supposed to like boys, let alone girls. I was supposed to be a good girl, go to school, go to church, get good grades, and keep my mouth shut about whatever I felt…because after all, being saved had nothing to do with feelings, right?

Being saved had so many restrictions even then that I would come to question; I wasn't supposed to listen to secular music, but I loved Luther Vandross. I wasn't supposed to wear pants, but I played basketball for my high school team. I wasn't supposed to go to the movies or dances, but I loved The Color Purple, and could actually dance pretty well. My friends had boyfriends, were having sex, and a couple were even having babies. I truly had no desire to be with any boys in an intimate fashion, but daydreamed about holding my friend's hand, holding her tight …what was I doing? What was I thinking? "Lord, get these impure thoughts out of my head, because I'm saved and living for you!!"

Fast forward to 1992. I was now seventeen, a senior in high school and really having feelings intensified for my friend. She actually succeeded in making me melt! We were both a part of the Black Student Union at school and one day, during a moment after finishing a task for the organization, she leaned in and kissed me on my cheek. I blushed to no end, but immediately began hearing in my head the voices of preachers, my peers and some family members condemning homosexuals. "Am I gay?" I asked myself. No way! I thought. I'm saved and can't be! I remember my uncle telling me that my mother was bisexual and that she was going to hell for that and several other sins. I knew I didn't want to go to hell. Back then, I didn't know those verses in Jeremiah: *"Before I formed thee, I knew thee…"* It never occurred to me that God knew exactly who I was, and what I was. I was always taught about becoming a new creature in Christ, and that I had to change in order to be made right. I couldn't think carnally at all. While we are supposed to love one another, I couldn't show my love to the one who captured my earthly heart.

Years later, I began the process of coming out. I was told that I was demon possessed, that I had no place in church because I had a girlfriend, who ironically, fought with me frequently because I spent more time in church doing God's work than I did with her. I was so torn. I loved God with every fiber of my being, but I was being told that He didn't love me. I faced homophobia within my family here in New York (where I would eventually relocate), homophobia in church where I continued to serve, homophobia in the streets and homophobia at work. I began slipping away from God, walking away from the only constant I had in my life, just because I had been foolish enough to believe that He didn't love me.

A late night conversation with God in 2009:

"Child of mine, I am going to use you to reach My people."
"Lord, not me. I can't." I said.

"Child of mine, I am going to use you to send a message of love."

"But God, I'm not worthy. They will not listen to me. No one will receive Your message through me. Don't You know who and what I am? I know You love me, but the world does not!" I said.

"Child of mine, before I formed you, I knew you. I know exactly who you are. I made you. I have people for you to reach that will listen. Just trust Me."

"But I'm scared, LORD." I said.

"I have not given you a spirit of fear, but of power. Trust in ME."

Even after having this conversation with God, even after He sent a messenger to confirm what He said, I ran like hell. I was serving at a traditional church at this time, and the message came from a very radical person. Someone who didn't fit the norm. Someone who was a lot like me. Gay. Saved. Living for God. I saw Him living within from the moment I laid eyes on her. Even after receiving the message, I went on living as normal, serving at a traditional church as normal, getting scandalized for being gay, as usual. I was living within the norms of what the church was proclaiming they were supposed to be, yet feeling as if they were acting Pharisaic.

After a while, I grew tired of leaving the house of God worse than how I went in. I was ready to give up. But, I heard His voice again, telling me to leave this Pharisaic traditional place and *"go where I will lead you."* I listened. God would send two more messengers. Similar to the first, they were a lot like me too. Gay. Saved. Anointed.

Called to minister. Still, I hesitated. Then the Word of the Lord came to me:

4 Now the word of the LORD came to me, saying,
5 "Before I formed you in the womb I knew you,
and before you were born I consecrated you;
I appointed you a prophet to the nations."
6 Then I said, "Ah, Lord GOD! Behold, I do not know how to
speak, for I am only a youth." 7 But the LORD said to me,
"Do not say, 'I am only a youth'
for to all to whom I send you, you shall go,
and whatever I command you, you shall speak.
8 Do not be afraid of them,
for I am with you to deliver you,
declares the LORD."
9 Then the LORD put out his hand and touched my mouth. And
the LORD said to me,
"Behold, I have put my words in your mouth.

I understood. God knew exactly what He was doing when He made me. He knew exactly who HE would need for me to reach before I could even fathom the thought. He knew my capabilities, my weaknesses, from before I was born. He knew each and every trial and tribulation I would endure in my life - rape, molestation, domestic violence, suffering ridicule and being ostracized from family and communities that were supposed to love, protect and support me. He ordained all of it so I could endure and live to tell about it, so that I could help someone else that has gone through the things I endured.

Why did he do it? Because He knows why I am here. He knows the work I am to do here on earth for Him. And most of all, He knows me. And loves me for me.

WHEN LOVING YOU IS HURTING ME
Pastor Lee Andrew Wright
Kingdom Building Victorious Church
Brooklyn, NY

What happens when you find yourself making foolish decisions, all in the name of love? When you have extended yourself to others in so many ways, and it seems like the more you give the more they take and there is no true reciprocation, of that which you have so generously provided?

What happens when you receive that knock on the door, after you promised yourself that the last time was the last time, now the person who holds your heart in their hand is standing on the doorsteps of your emotions, and you can't quite say *"no"* because the soul tie is so deep, that it seems that a very possible GOD can't seem to help you get out of this, what seems to be impossible, situation.

We have all been there, in the place where we couldn't quite seem to *"measure up."* When misplaced love caused us for a brief moment to turn our backs on our confession and willingly take temptation by the hand and say as the songstress Anita Baker puts it ,*"Lead Me Into Love. "*

The question now becomes: *Is this really love?* Is this the type of love God desired for me to have or is this the only love I've ever known? Are my nights so lonely and long that I have to give myself away to be used and abused by anyone and everyone?

Just to feel empty, abandoned and depleted, just to hear those three empty words *I LOVE YOU!*

True love causes you to cry tears of joy, not tears of pain, bitterness and sorrow. True love reaches beyond the satin sheets of fornication, masturbation and self-humiliation. Love, the GOD kind of Love will call you just to say *"Hello,"* without looking for a rendezvous. What happens when loving you starts to hurt me? When my dreams become nightmares because I shared my secrets with the wrong one? Now I've become so impenetrable that even though physically I'm no longer chaste, my heart becomes so bitter that it is clasped.

What happens when loving you is hurting me? *I wake up!* I take a retrospective look within myself, to forgive myself, because I gave myself away, to someone who really didn't love me. I am no longer giddy or beguiled. You took my heart and you raped it. Yeah I trusted you, when on a date with you and you took possession over that which you did not own, and when we were through, all you could do is whisper in my ear those same three empty words, *"I Love You."*

That's it! I see! What you taught me wasn't love. It wasn't love at all. It was a manipulated attempt to destroy my soul. You taught me how to speak in tongues and feel ecstasy, that I was nothing if you weren't next to me. You took my power and revealed my mysteries, but when it was over, you wouldn't even speak to me.

I thought that my tears would fade away, with the promises of you'll be back someday, so when you called I jumped…and I jumped…paid your child support while I jumped…and jumped. Until one day the bank called to say my account was overdrawn and the phone calls stopped and the pain began again, because you had me thinking that no matter what I say, what I believe and what I do, that I'd be bankrupt if I didn't have you.

But one day I bumped into love. Just when I thought I was going to die, true love stepped in smiled and said *"Let me introduce myself…I am God. My friends call Me the Most High!"* After some time getting to know God and removing the pains of my past, God taught me to look at you as a joker, which caused me to laugh.

God taught me something that you never did. See, I was doing all those things but still I couldn't live. I couldn't live, because I was wrapped up in the perception of what love should be. That's when I realized that loving you was hurting me.

See God taught me that Love never gives up; Love cares more for others than for self. That Love doesn't want what Love doesn't have and that Love doesn't strut, have a big ego, forces itself on or takes advantage of others. That Love isn't always *"me"* first and flies off the handle. Doesn't keep the score on the sins of others. Doesn't revel when others beg or plead. Love takes pleasure in truth and puts up with *anything!* And by the way *My* Love trusts in God and always looks for the best.

Love told me to never look back, to keep pressing ahead and that the Love we share, it will never end.

So thank you for the memories, without you, I didn't know I could be this strong. And with heartfelt gratitude, I say..."*So long!*"

 Signed Sincerely,

I Got My Heart Back!

At The Table

for black bois

Danez Smith
Madison, WI

they say there's suga in your tank
& everyone prayin you learn

to hide the candy shop in your voice
to dust the sweet off your slim shoulders

you double-dutch better than the best girl
taught them how to make their hips a compass
 shake it to the east, shake it to the west

you mama's head is low like she mournin something
her feet sweep round the house

like she tryin to lose track of you.
they all stare at you striding, switching

it off is something you can't do
God gave you a rhythm

damn if you don't dance it.

Danez Smith is a Cave Canem Fellow and two time Pushcart
nominee living in Madison, WI. Currently a college advisor at
the University of Wisconsin, he has been writing poems since
the age of ten. His work has been published or is
forthcoming in PANK, Anti-Southern Indiana Review,
decomP, the Collagist, and other journals. For more
information, visit http://danezsmith.org

LISTENING FOR THE SOUND:
My Journey Toward Authenticity
Rev. Dawnn M. Brumfield
Chicago, IL

Some years ago I was given a book entitled *Do You Think I'm Beautiful* and I was struck by the title. I had often pondered this question: physical beauty is a highly valued, perhaps *the most highly valued* commodity in the American culture. Keats wrote about the association of Truth with Beauty, but in my experience, the prominent association of beauty was with self-worth. I found myself equating self-worth with physical appearance. From that book I began to learn how physical beauty is a social construct negotiated or reaffirmed in social interaction.

The culture tells us about our standards of beauty: ideal weight and height; hair, eye, and skin color; hairstyle and make-up; clothing and posture. The construct varies according to culture: what is considered beautiful in one setting is ugly in another. For example, to a society facing famine, a comparably heavy person can be seen as both healthy and beautiful; to a society marked by excess, the thinner the model, the more beautiful she is considered to be. But, the social constructs are naturalized; we cannot escape our cultural conditioning, and so we judge ourselves by arbitrary standards. And we do more than judge. We strive to meet the cultural ideal, through diet and exercise, make-up and hair dye, Botox and surgery. Should we fail to seek attaining this goal, we are given cultural warning: we are abnormal. And should we seek the means of attainment, we need look no further than a grocery store check-out to find magazines that describe how physical beauty can be obtained. We are bombarded with images in movies, television programs, commercial advertisements and the like that not only show us the ideal, they show us how we have failed to meet that ideal, and how we can meet it, if we simply buy the right toothpaste or use the right lipstick. But the quick fix doesn't work. The harder we try to achieve the beauty marketed to us, the more imperfect we feel ourselves to be, and so the lower our esteem sinks. The chase for beauty can become so extreme that even after some of us resort to crash diets, medication or surgery, we are still never satisfied. The skin could be smoother, the abs tighter, the hair shinier, and so we pursue an impossible ideal. Though I've lost a lot of weight and am now much healthier, at nearly 430 lbs., which I believe, was my highest weight at one point (I stopped weighing because it was too embarrassing), I was always trying to fit in. The irony was that I was always trying to hide myself but my size made that task nearly impossible. So I adapted and made myself invisible. I'd do the behind the scenes work and shrink in the presence of others. It was a very lonely place; I just wanted to belong.

I was not happy with me because I was constantly comparing myself to others---and sometimes I still do. As a young child---and sometimes even as an adult---I wanted so badly to be accepted. I wanted so badly for people to see me and know me. But the entire time I never searched once to discover how God sees me. For me, at that time, it didn't matter how God saw me. I was already saved. I had made the decision to 'turn or burn,' so as far as God and I were concerned I was good. My love for God was intact. My love from other people---as far as I could see it---was mostly there. But, my love for myself was still missing. I was consumed with all that I had done wrong. I was shamed by all that was done wrong to me. I wanted to see me and love me as God saw me and loved me. I was searching. This was a profound insight for me. For as long as I have been on this journey toward authenticity I've been searching for an integrated love. That is, to see me and love me as God sees me and loves me. It is a journey toward my authentic.

If I were writing a book I would write about how I once fell in love. The introduction would talk about how the love grew over time. I would talk about how I knew immediately that I was in love. In chapter one I would include the story about how we met. There would be at least one section that highlighted the late night phone conversations; there would be a section for the fight and a section about making up. It would probably also mention how we met. It would also say that this love awakened in me was shared with another woman. My relationship with my partner, Denise, has helped to shape my pastoral identity. It forced me to reflect on how I understood my call. The conflict I imagined between my love for God, my relationship with my partner and my service in full-time ministry increased my discipline for prayer. I was always in communication with God about my perceived clash. For a long time I was trying to reconcile a deep love that I share with this woman and how it might affect my relationship with God. I wondered how it would affect my work in ministry.

In the book, *A Whosoever Church: Welcoming Lesbians and Gay Men Into African American Congregations*, Rev. Dr. Jacquelyn Grant was asked, "What kind of advice do you have for African American lesbians and gay men who are trying to find a church or who are thinking about leaving the church (133)?" Her response, "I usually recommend that they spend more time-which can be liberating, but not necessarily so- searching for a church where they can feel comfortable…I don't think that gays and lesbians always have to leave traditional churches to find comfort, but I suppose that more and more of them are becoming increasingly frustrated with the traditional context…my advice most times is, 'well, if you leave the church, who's going to be there to fight; who's going to be there to struggle; who's going to be there to change things?" I appreciated the question and I welcomed Dr. Grant's response. This was precisely my struggle. When I first admitted that I was committed to living a full, balanced life, that is, fully engaged to my Call as a pastor and completely connected to my relationship with my partner I was ready to 'leave the church.' Though I wanted to continue my service to God and God's people I was willing to 'turn in my collar' because I was painfully aware of the treatment of the LGBTQ community in many Christian faith traditions. The thought of leaving, however, made my heart grieve. I enjoy my work as a minister. I love that God calls me to connect and journey with others as they transform. My heart could not bear the idea of walking away. So, instead I committed to staying and engaging with my colleagues in the work of reframing the spiritual journey of Christian faith. This was God's gift of love to me.

The journey is not complete. God continues to call me. God beckons me to come. God's love for me is complete. I desire to respond to that love by loving myself completely. I want to experience the same kind of love for myself. For me part of the journey toward loving myself is to continue to seek, search and find what Howard Thurman calls "The Sound of the Genuine." He says,

"There is in every person something that waits and listens for the sound of the genuine in herself…nobody like you has ever been born and no one like you will ever be born again---you are the only one…don't be deceived and thrown off by all of the noises that are a part even of your dreams and your ambitions that you don't hear the sound of the genuine in you. You may be famous. You may be whatever the other ideals are which are a part of this generation, but you know you don't have the foggiest notion of who you are, where you are going, what you want." (The Sound of the Genuine, Baccalaureate Address, University of Indianapolis)

This is what I am trying to fulfill. I am searching for the sound of my voice. I am a daughter, a sister, a partner and a friend. I am a pastor, a student, and a teacher. I am all of these things because I hear the sound of the genuine in myself. And I love hearing that sound, which at times is garbled and distorted; I am learning to be okay with that, too. But, the best part of it all is that if I am quiet enough and we can trust each other enough to move past some of our otherness, I can hear the sound of the genuine in you, too.

THE WHOLE TRUTH AND NOTHING BUT THE TRUTH

Pastor Shannon Gresham
His Coming Ministries
Baltimore, Maryland

The church is often in a whimsical state. We are on a mission making disciples and growing the congregation in number that we often forget about growing the Kingdom in quality. The clergy is concerned with wearing the best robes and driving the fanciest cars. The burden of the new multi-million dollar sanctuary just erected from the ground often rests on the shoulders of below average blue collar workers just trying to make ends meet but believing in a vision greater than their wallet. When I think of what modern day church has become, I am speechless. We parade around with our degrees on the wall of our offices and create little servants out of innocent people, just wanting to change their life through a relationship with Christ. The modern day church has become an occupation for those who did exceptionally well in communications class or popped straight "A's" in psychology class and for those who are looking to showcase their findings on the unsuspecting. Moreover, those who couldn't find acceptance in the mainstream church, hence, the traditional unwelcoming heterosexist confines of conventional religion, are submitting resumes and joining fellowships to be the next Bishop, Overseer, Senior Pastor, etc of the next church plant catering to those of the LGBT community. The same way we were held in bondage, the same statues that kept us enslaved to the Law, the same set of rules that made us live legalistically and not in liberty are the same rules we turn and twist to spiritually brainwash our predecessors.

What is the purpose of my exposé'? What is the purpose for this literary piece that seems to target the church in a negative way? The truth of the matter is I am a Pastor. I came up in the same system that was used to enslave. My friends are Overseers, Bishops, Apostles, and Pastors who are rising up churches in this hour. Many of us have truly understood what it means to be called to the Nations. We understand that the system that we criticized, the system that limited us, the system that persecuted us based on who we chose to love is the system that we CAME OUT OF. We teach our congregations what it means to COME OUT of bondage... To COME OUT of religion...To COME OUT of limitations...To COME OUT of man-made rules and regulations... To COME OUT of slavery...We realize that COMING OUT is not just a process of sexuality, but it is a process of spirituality. I encourage those of us who took several years to reconcile our sexuality with our spirituality to begin to reconcile our spirituality with our religiosity. We must introduce the saints to the liberty which exists in Christ Jesus. We are too busy looking for people to have flaws and judging their relationship with God based on worldly standards. We judge based on physical appearances, social status, moral infractions, and even a person's past. God looks at the HEART. When we begin to see with the eyes of God and love with the heart of God, people will come into a saving knowledge of who Jesus is and see us as the servants of Christ that we are. They are too busy looking at us and their eyes are not focused on him. I'm quick to say, our God is a jealous God. If we put anything before him, including ourselves, we are in a dangerous place. It's a sad thing when on Sunday morning, the Saints are more concerned with pleasing the Pastor than pleasing their God...I'm just saying. The whole truth and nothing but the truth is... Let's get the religion out of spirituality and allow people to truly COME OUT of Egypt into the land God has promised.

NOTHING CAN SEPARATE YOU FROM GOD'S LOVE!

"No, in all these things we are more than conquerors through him who loved us. For I am sure that neither death nor life, nor angels nor rulers, nor things present nor things to come, nor powers, nor height nor depth, nor anything else in all creation, will be able to separate us from the love of God in Christ Jesus our Lord."

Romans 8:37-39

#onward/Creator
Denise L. Hill
Chicago, IL

When I reflect on my younger years I wish I had the courage then to articulate my feelings. I wish I had learned to express myself in a way where it conveyed who I am without compromising the dynamic of my family. I don't place blame or have shame from the dysfunction of my family relationships; hardship is how I learned to survive. Now I accept responsibility to stop the history; I refuse to allow the cycle to continue.

I was built strong; I was made to persevere through what many of my family members probably couldn't deal with. I had self-sustainability in spite of what people felt; I was determined to just be me despite what culture said different. My sexuality placed me in a position where it helped me to see the world around me. But, I had to explore and open myself to looking inward and realize that I am human. I have been hurt, isolated, and walked away from by the closest people in my life. For years I continued to replay past encounters and relive experiences that inhibited me from forming healthy relationships. Onward I know I will make mistakes but I am making a conscious decision to be transformed in an effort to keep moving forward.

I have a deep need to connect. When I evaluate and reflect on my subconscious expressions, my need to connect is even more evident. This need is a desire to join with something less tangible than color pencil to paper or eye piece to a camera. Instead it is a strong urge to create meaning from my experiences and to use my gifts to make an impact on the world.

I use my poetry to tell a story. The words represent where and how I link to life. Not long ago I began a journey of exploration not knowing where it would take me but trusting that guidance, and a strong, personal force would lead me. I was ready to move #onward. My internal grief led me to a space where I began to use poetry to process and integrate my feelings and thoughts; this was my way to create, connect and belong. On March 1, 2012 my Mom, at the age of fifty-one, died from an infection initiated by her bone marrow transplant. At that time I wanted to disconnect from everything but deep down I knew I had to grasp a perspective different of my reality. My mother was gone. But the memories of my relationship with my mom---one that still continues despite her death---and reflections on the relationships I share with others made me realize that detaching was not an option. As months passed I gained a sense of my own truth; writing and art became a therapeutic outlet that gave expression to my feelings, my sorrow. Through writing and creating I began to see how some of my life experiences---growing pains, awkward friendships, and unhealthy personal relationships---participated in muting my voice. Now I am ready to move #onward.

Creator

As a creator, made from the Creator
An educator never took the time to grab insight into this
young child's development as an artist

They deemed her to fail
Discarded
and disregarded that this child may be an initiator
because her hands did the talking

She invents visions behind words of aspirations
and thoughts that were conceptualized by intellects
But disregarded because her words blurred across the
lines
and mathematics didn't add up

Set aside for "special classes"
not knowing someone special was sitting in the class
Abstract
and not conformed to the natural norm

Never thought this child could be a creator
but SHE IS!

WHEN LOVE ENDS

(Angel-Angelo Mettoyer writing as) Blackfoot Marine
Chicago, IL

It is truly hard to know or even seriously comprehend how incredibly viciously love can hurt when the person that you were once in love with no longer continues to love you back. You find yourself doubting everything about that person as well as the very nature of the relationship that you were in together. When love ends it hurts. The holding each other intimately in each other's arms with so much love care and affection, stops. The softly spoken all night and all day conversations that you would have with each other just to hear each other's voices, stops. The sweet delicate sultry passionate seemingly never ending kisses that you thought you could not live without, stops. The very act of making love and having sex together gets relegated to being just a memory.

When your present and your future together are no more, you suddenly find yourself sitting, walking, riding, eating and sleeping alone. Blind-sided and in shock and embarrassed, you involuntarily stare into open space thinking about everything but not really wanting to speak with anyone about how brutally crushed and nakedly vulnerable you honestly feel. You most especially do not want to discuss the hurt and the betrayal and devastating gut-punching heart-wrenching loss that you feel because you feel so foolish for having risked loving anyone at all. How could someone smart like you fall into the insidiously cruel joke and trap of falling in love over and over again and again? You pick yourself apart and wonder whether or not you are even worthy and deserving of being truly deeply and forever loved by anyone ever. You feel entirely devalued. You can't really sleep and you don't want to eat. You walk and pace in circles and you sit hopeless and defeated in the middle of your bed. You stop answering your phone. You avoid the internet and you only go outside to retrieve and mail and to take out the garbage. The words from your friends which should comfort you somehow seem to fall on deaf ears. You retreat to self-imposed isolation.

In your mind without thinking and not meaning to have a crisis of faith you ask God, "Why me Lord? What have I ever done to deserve this much pain? Why won't anyone really love me? Why won't my relationships last? If you truly love me Lord, why would you let them do this to me?" You regret it and you apologize to God and you ask for His forgiveness almost as soon as you think those things because you quickly realize that perhaps your thoughts could possibly be construed as blaming God and accusing God for failing to protect you from yourself and others who prey on your feelings and insecurities and lie to you by declaring their complete and eternal and unflinching love to you.

Heavenly Father, I love you, Abba. It's hard to breathe and I feel like I'm dying. Lord God, I know that you love me please help me get through this because I just can't bear it alone. Please don't let me go through this alone.

I need you Lord. Father I need you so very much.
Please help me. Help me to survive this. Help me to
live and not die.

Every human relationship has its own trajectory, its own
natural progression and its own certainty of ending. Be
it through old age and infirmity, war, death, betrayal,
legal separation, divorce or whatever at some point all
human physical relationships end. That said, it is
important that we fully comprehend that because we are
primarily spiritual beings we will almost always have
some sort of a spiritual heart based link with our past
true loves, each one of them retains a place in our hearts
whether we want them to or not.

Part of being a fully human well-functioning sexually
active adult is the often unspoken obligation of our own
personal responsibility to love wisely and to closely guard
our own hearts; to not be careless as to who and what
we permit in our lives; to not be cavalier about sharing
ourselves with others and to not move so fast when it
comes to giving ourselves away. We can't protect
ourselves from everything or everyone but we can
certainly do better than what we've done. We must be
much more spiritually and intellectually selective as to
our choice of mates and not just settle on someone
because we find them physically attractive and or
sexually stimulating. We must love wisely.

Even in the midst and the turmoil of our angst over lost
love it is important that we know, understand and
believe that we will love again no matter how much it

hurts right now. Over time God will heal our hearts and get us through this, God always does because the most important love that we'll ever truly need, we already have in the Lord. Although we feel pain deeply and it cuts us to the quick, we are not the hothouse flowers that we often wrongly perceive ourselves to be, God made us much more resilient and a whole lot stronger than that. We've been designed to learn, change and adapt which intrinsically enables us to overcome a great many seemingly insurmountable obstacles and challenges as well as some life threatening events that we find ourselves faced with. Untested faith has no value. Even when our insomnia producing, mind numbing, vomit triggering heartache makes us feel as if we're choking to death, these fiery trials of life inadvertently serve to humble, forge and strengthen us to make us much more suitable for God's use.

Regardless of our gender status or sexual orientation, we must believe in ourselves and know that we can do better and we must hold fast to the knowledge that no matter how dismally infinitivally bleak things might look right now, God will provide. No door closes without God opening another. It's okay to cry. Go ahead and cry but be encouraged for just as sure as the sun will set tonight and rise again tomorrow, we will survive our broken hearts. The Holy Spirit of God will get us through this rough crossing for God promises to never leave or forsake us. We are all His children and we are greatly loved by Him. All we need to do is believe in Him and to pray to Him in the name of His Son Jesus Christ for the loving mercy of His grace.

MY FEAR IN LIVING
Min. Keston O. Lee
New York, NY

I was scared to try cause I was scared to fail

I was scared to die cause I'm scared of going to hell

I was scared to kiss scared to hug

I was scared of sex cause I was scared to be touched

I was scared to look cause I was scared of what I'd find

I was scared to fly cause I was scared to crash

I was scared of me so I was scared of you

I was scared to move on so I lived in my past

I was scared of fighting cause I'm scared to bleed

I was scared of love cause I was scared they would leave

I was scared of drugs cause I might get hooked I'm even

scared to drink cause I will go off the hook

I was scared to learn cause I was scared of the truth

I was scared to gain weight so I was scared of food

I was scared to think that the church will drop me

I'm scared to think of my ministry vision flopping

At The Table

This may sound silly but it's true

So if you reading this don't pretend it ain't you too

We are all afraid of something here on earth

Cause you ain't human without fear

I was scared to start cause I was scared I'd quit

I was scared to swim cause I was scared I'd sink

I'm scared of fame so I lay low

I was scared that people wouldn't like me so I let my

defenses show

Scared to grow up cause I'm scared of getting old

Scared of the dark and scared of being alone

I was scared of war I was scared of jail...

....until spending a night there

And, until I found God for myself I was scared of hell

Scared to share my secrets cause I was scared you'd tell

These were my Fears of Living as a Gay Black Male.

YOU ARE EQUAL IN THE BODY OF CHRIST

"In Christ's family there can be no division into Jew and non-Jew, slave and free, male and female. Among us you are all equal. That is, we are all in a common relationship with Jesus Christ."

Galatians 3:28

I KNOW
For LGBTQi Youth Considering Suicide
Susan A. Webley-Cox

I know.
I know that you're tired
Of putting up the front and
Hiding behind a representative
Of your true self
A slave with no emancipation in sight
You'd gladly risk the possible infection
Of cutting off your own foot
To be you
Just. Be. YOU.
But you can't.

Baby, I know.

I know what it's like
To be a ghost
In a full room
And not fit anywhere
And not belong to anything
And not feel loved by anyone.

I know what it's like
To have to suck it up
And smile a smile
Perfectly crafted
To hide the blackness

That's slowly replacing the blood flowing through your
veins
To mask the stench of your dying spirit
As it gives birth to doubt
Low esteem
Self-loathing
Self-deprecation

And you start to believe
That you are nothing
That you don't matter
That you aren't worthy
 Of living

Baby, I know.

I know you just want it to stop
You want the pain to stop
The torment to stop
The hate to stop
The dismissal to stop
The abuse to stop
The bullying to stop
JUST
STOP!

It hurts and
No one understands you
And you're screaming
But no one hears you
Your family has turned their back
The church has condemned you to hell

And you deserve it, right?
I mean you are not supposed to have those kinds of
feelings anyway
And it serves you right because you are an abomination
anyway
And you deserve to suffer because you're acting
unnaturally anyway
And who cares if you die because you'd be doing
humanity a huge favor anyway
After all, that would mean one less lesbian, gay, bisexual,
transgendered or questioning youth to contend with…

So with tears in your eyes
You begin to look at that bottle of pills
Or the razor
Or the knife
As redemption
Embracing death as your savior
Justifying your demise as
Releasing the world of the burden
Of you…
I know.

But I also know that you were created by a God who
knew you before you were formed in your mother's
belly. He knew just how special you would be, that you
would love differently from everyone else. You are
unique in His eyes, to Him, your life is precious. When
man tells you otherwise, remember that you DO matter,
you ARE worthy and YOU ARE LOVED by God.
 Nothing can ever separate you from His love.

NOTHING! Hold on to that. Keep telling yourself that. And if you need me, I am here. I
will talk to you, pray with you and will do my best to help you affirm the wonderful and beautiful human being that you are. Take it from a survivor. It will get better. I PROMISE you it will.

At The Table
The Contributors:

Elder Freddie Washington III

Elder Maurice L. Robinson

Stephfon L. Guidry

Overseer Yvonne M. Harrison

Rev. Dawnn M. Brumfield

Jerrold Yam

Deacon Shamayara M. Woodson, MHS

Rev. Dr. L. Christi Hunter

Ferrin Mitchell

Isis Pickens

Rev. Leslie Oliver

Cole Thomas

Asher Kolieboi

Rev. E. Taylor Doctor

Min. Janet Lafontaine

Pastor Lee Andrew Wright

Danez Smith

Pastor Shannon Gresham

Denise L. Hill

(Angel-Angelo Mettoyer writing as) Blackfoot Marine

Min. Keston O. Lee

Susan A. Webley-Cox

About Susan

Susan A. Webley-Cox is a mother, daughter, wife, writer, editor and graphic designer. A minister of the Gospel at NYC based Restoration Temple Ministries (where Overseer Yvonne M. Harrison is the Senior Pastor) Susan serves as Director of the Youth & Young Adult Department and Christian Education, respectively. She also sits on the board of the church's Liturgical & Fine Arts Ministry.

In 2002, Susan launched community award nominated SABLE Magazine, a publication for Women of Color in the LGBTQ community, which had the distinction of being the first of its kind online. During its six year run, the e-zine covered a mirage of topics, providing articles and features that were designed to feed the mind and nourish the soul.

Susan is the founder of The Exousia Book Club and is currently developing AFFIRMED: Where You Have a Seat at the Table, an online magazine/community for LGBTQi Believers and their allies in the Body of Christ.

She resides in Brooklyn, NY with her wife and partner in ministry, Millie Cox.

Publisher's Note

Thank you so much for your purchase of this rare and ground-breaking book compiled and edited by Susan A. Webley-Cox!

I am so very honored to be the publishing house for this truly inspirational work.

If you enjoyed reading At the Table: Words of Faith, Affirmation and Inspiration for LGBT Believers of Color, please visit our website for our new, featured and upcoming publications.

About Azaan:

Azaan Kamau started Glover Lane Press in the summer of 2000 to give a voice to poets, journalists, and writers worldwide. Azaan and Glover Lane Press have helped countless individuals publish and distribute media in print and in digital formats.

As a woman, one of Azaan's publishing goals is to focus on marginalized or over-looked communities of writers, poets, artists, and photographers. Azaan feels everyone has a story that must be heard or recorded. Another important goal is to use the proceeds from sales of Azaan's books to improve the lives of people around the world. Azaan's books and her companies will feed the hungry, house the homeless, heal the sick, educate and eradicate disease, etc!

At The Table

www. gloverlanepress.webs.com
www.letterstomybully.webs.com
www.Facebook.com/Gloverlanepress

For an entire list of our print books and electronic books, you can also visit us on www.Amazon.com

Again, thank you for your purchase!

I May Be....

I may be a butch and even gay, but The LORD is my shepherd; I shall not want.

They may slay me with their words, and bitter hate-filled lies, but He maketh me to lie down in green pastures: he leadeth me beside the still waters.

They carry signs that shout, God Hates Fags, but He restoreth my soul: he leadeth me in the paths of righteousness for his name's sake.

They don't understand me because Yea, though I walk through the valley of the shadow of death, I will fear no evil: for thou art with me; thy rod and thy staff they comfort me.

They tried to bully me into self-hate even though, Thou preparest a table before me in the presence of mine enemies: thou anointest my head with oil; my cup runneth over.

I may be a stud, but Surely goodness and mercy shall follow me all the days of my life: and I will dwell in the house of the LORD forever.

Azaan Kamau

At The Table

CPSIA information can be obtained at www.ICGtesting.com
Printed in the USA
BVOW05s1836050814

361778BV00003B/172/P